3 0183 02542 2187

D1270714

21ST CENTURY HEALTH
AND WELLNESS

The Reproductive System

Regina Avraham

Introduction by C. Everett Koop, M.D., Sc.D.
Former Surgeon General, U.S. Public Health Service

Foreword by Sandra Thurman
Director, Office of National AIDS Policy, The White House

CHELSEA HOUSE PUBLISHERS
Philadelphia

The goal of *21ST CENTURY HEALTH AND WELLNESS* is to provide general information in the ever-changing areas of physiology, psychology, and related medical issues. The titles in this series are not intended to take the place of the professional advice of a physician or other health-care professional.

Chelsea House Publishers
EDITOR IN CHIEF: Stephen Reginald
PRODUCTION MANAGER: Pamela Loos
ART DIRECTOR: Sara Davis
DIRECTOR OF PHOTOGRAPHY: Judy Hasday
MANAGING EDITOR: James D. Gallagher
SENIOR PRODUCTION EDITOR: J. Christopher Higgins
ASSISTANT EDITOR: Anne Hill
PRODUCTION SERVICES: Pre-Press Company, Inc.
COVER DESIGNER/ILLUSTRATOR: Emiliano Begnardi

The Chelsea House World Wide Web site address is http://www.chelseahouse.com

1 3 5 7 9 8 6 4 2

Library of Congress Cataloging-in-Publication Data applied for:

ISBN 0-7910-5988-X

CONTENTS

PREVENTION AND EDUCATION: THE KEYS TO GOOD HEALTH

C. Everett Koop, M.D., Sc.D.
FORMER SURGEON GENERAL,
U.S. Public Health Service

The issue of health education has received particular attention in recent years because of the presence of AIDS in the news. But our response to this particular tragedy points up a number of broader issues that doctors, public health officials, educators, and the public face. In particular, it spotlights the importance of sound health education for citizens of all ages.

Over the past 35 years, this country has been able to achieve dramatic declines in the death rates from heart disease, stroke, accidents, and—for people under the age of 45—cancer. Today, Americans generally eat better and take better care of themselves than ever before. Thus, with the help of modern science and technology, they have a better chance of surviving serious—even catastrophic—illnesses. In 1996, the life expectancy of Americans reached an all-time high of 76.1 years. That's the good news.

The flip side of this advance has special significance for young adults. According to a report issued in 1998 by the U.S. Department of Health and Human Services, levels of wealth and education in the United States are directly correlated with our population's health. The more money Americans make and the more years of schooling they have, the better their health will be. Furthermore, income inequality increased in the U.S. between 1970 and 1996. Basically, the rich got richer—people in high income brackets had greater increases in the amount of money made than did those at low income levels. In addition, the report indicated that children under 18 are more likely to live in poverty than the population as a whole.

Family income rises with each higher level of education for both men and women from every ethnic and racial background. Life expectancy, too, is related to family income. People with lower incomes tend to die at younger ages than people from more affluent homes. What all this means is that health is a factor of wealth and education, both of which need to be improved for all Americans if the promise of life, liberty, and the pursuit of happiness is to include an equal chance for good health.

The health of young people is further threatened by violent death and injury, alcohol and drug abuse, unwanted pregnancies, and sexually transmitted diseases. Adolescents are particularly vulnerable because they are beginning to explore their own sexuality and perhaps to experiment with drugs and alcohol. We need to educate young people to avoid serious dangers to their health. The price of neglect is high.

Even for the population as a whole, health is still far from what it could be. Why? Most death and disease are attributed to four broad elements: inadequacies in the health-care system, behavioral factors or unhealthy lifestyles, environmental hazards, and human biological factors. These categories are also influenced by individual resources. For example, low birth weight and infant mortality are more common among the children of less educated mothers. Likewise, women with more education are more likely to obtain prenatal care during pregnancy. Mothers with fewer than 12 years of education are almost 10 times more likely to smoke during pregnancy—and new studies find excessive aggression later in life as well as other physical ailments among the children of smokers. In short, poor people with less education are more likely to smoke cigarettes, which endangers health and shortens the life span. About a third of the children who begin smoking will eventually have their lives cut short because of this practice.

Similarly, poor children are exposed more often to environmental lead, which causes a wide range of physical and mental problems. Sedentary lifestyles are also more common among teens with lower family income than among wealthier adolescents. Being overweight—a condition associated with physical inactivity as well as excessive caloric intake—is also more common among poor, non-Hispanic, white adolescents. Children from rich families are more likely to have health insurance. Therefore, they are more apt to receive vaccinations and other forms of early preventative medicine and treatment. The bottom line is that kids from lower income groups receive less adequate health care.

To be sure, some diseases are still beyond the control of even the most advanced medical techniques that our richest citizens can afford. Despite yearnings that are as old as the human race itself, there is no "fountain of youth" to prevent aging and death. Still, solutions are available for many of the problems that undermine sound health. In a word, that solution is prevention. Prevention, which includes health promotion and education, can save lives, improve the quality of life, and, in the long run, save money.

In the United States, organized public health activities and preventative medicine have a long history. Important milestones include the improvement of sanitary procedures and the development of pasteurized milk in the late-19th century, and the introduction in the mid-20th century of effective vaccines against polio, measles, German measles, mumps, and other once-rampant diseases. Internationally, organized public health efforts began on a wide-scale basis with the International Sanitary Conference of 1851, to which 12 nations sent representatives. The World Health Organization, founded in 1948, continues these efforts under the aegis of the United Nations, with particular emphasis on combating communicable diseases and the training of health-care workers.

Despite these accomplishments, much remains to be done in the field of prevention. For too long, we have had a medical system that is science and technology-based, and focuses essentially on illness and mortality. It is now patently obvious that both the social and the economic costs of such a system are becoming insupportable.

Implementing prevention and its corollaries, health education and health promotion, is the job of several groups of people. First, the medical and scientific professions need to continue basic scientific research, and here we are making considerable progress. But increased concern with prevention will also have a decided impact on how primary-care doctors practice medicine. With a shift to health-based rather than morbidity-based medicine, the role of the "new physician" includes a healthy dose of patient education.

Second, practitioners of the social and behavioral sciences—psychologists, economists, and city planners along with lawyers, business leaders, and government officials—must solve the practical and ethical dilemmas confronting us: poverty, crime, civil rights, literacy, education, employment, housing, sanitation, environmental protection, health-care delivery systems, and so forth. All of these issues affect public health.

Third is the public at large. We consider this group to be important in any movement. Fourth, and the linchpin in this effort, is the public health profession: doctors, epidemiologists, teachers—who must harness the professional expertise of the first two groups and the common sense and cooperation of the third: the public. They must define the problems statistically and qualitatively and then help set priorities for finding solutions.

To a very large extent, improving health statistics is the responsibility of every individual. So let's consider more specifically what the role of the individual should be and why health education is so important. First, and most obviously, individuals can protect themselves from illness and injury and thus minimize the need for professional medical care. They can eat a nutritious diet; get adequate exercise; avoid tobacco, alcohol, and drugs; and take prudent steps to avoid accidents. The proverbial "apple a day keeps the doctor away" is not so far from the truth, after all.

Second, individuals should actively participate in their own medical care. They should schedule regular medical and dental checkups. If an illness or injury develops, they should know when to treat themselves and when to seek professional help. To gain the maximum benefit from any medical treatment, individuals must become partners in treatment. For instance, they should understand the effects and side effects of medications. I counsel young physicians that there is no such thing as too much information when talking with patients. But the corollary is the patient must know enough about the nuts and bolts of the healing process to understand what the doctor is telling him or her. That responsibility is at least partially the patient's.

Education is equally necessary for us to understand the ethical and public policy issues in health care today. Sometimes individuals will encounter these issues in making decisions about their own treatment or that of family members. Other citizens may encounter them as jurors in medical malpractice cases. But we all become involved, indirectly, when we elect our public officials, from school board members to the president. Should surrogate parenting be legal? To what extent is drug testing desirable, legal, or necessary? Should there be public funding for family planning, hospitals, various types of medical research, and medical care for the indigent? How should we allocate scant technological resources, such as kidney dialysis and organ transplants? What is the proper role of government in protecting the rights of patients?

What are the broad goals of public health in the United States today? The Public Health Service has defined these goals in terms of mortality, education, and health improvement. It identified 15 major concerns: controlling high blood pressure, improving family planning, pregnancy care and infant health, increasing the rate of immunization, controlling sexually transmitted diseases, controlling the presence of toxic agents or radiation in the environment, improving occupational safety and health, preventing accidents, promoting water fluoridation and dental health, controlling infectious diseases, decreasing smoking, decreasing alcohol and drug abuse, improving nutrition, promoting physical fitness and exercise, and controlling stress and violent behavior. Great progress has been made in many of these areas. For example, the report *Health, United States, 1998* indicates that in general, the workplace is safer today than it was a decade ago. Between 1980 and 1993, the overall death rate from occupational injuries dropped 45 percent to 4.2 deaths per 100,000 workers.

For healthy adolescents and young adults (ages 15 to 24), the specific goal defined by the Public Health Service was a 20% reduction in deaths, with a special focus on motor vehicle injuries as well as alcohol and drug abuse. For adults (ages 25 to 64), the aim was 25% fewer deaths, with a concentration on heart attacks, strokes, and cancers. In the 1999 National Drug Control Strategy, the White House Office of National Drug Control Policy echoed the Congressional goal of reducing drug use by 50 percent in the coming decade.

Smoking is perhaps the best example of how individual behavior can have a direct impact on health. Today cigarette smoking is recognized as the most important single preventable cause of death in our society. It is responsible for more cancers and more cancer deaths than any other known agent; is a prime risk factor for heart and blood vessel disease, chronic bronchitis, and emphysema; and is a frequent cause of complications in pregnancies and of babies born prematurely, underweight, or with potentially fatal respiratory and cardiovascular problems.

Since the release of the Surgeon General's first report on smoking in 1964, the proportion of adult smokers has declined substantially, from 43% in 1965 to 30.5% in 1985. The rate of cigarette smoking among adults declined from 1974 to 1995, but rates of decline were greater among the more educated. Since 1965, more than 50 million people have quit smoking. Although the rate of adult smoking has decreased, children and teenagers are smoking more. Researchers have also noted a disturbing correlation between underage smoking of cigarettes and later use of cocaine and heroin. Although there is still much work to be done if we are to become a "smoke free society," it is heartening to note that public health and public education efforts—such as warnings on cigarette packages, bans on broadcast advertising, removal of billboards advertising cigarettes, and anti-drug youth campaigns in the media— have already had significant effects.

In 1997, the first leveling off of drug use since 1992 was found in eighth graders, with marijuana use in the past month declining to 10 percent. The percentage of eighth graders who drink alcohol or smoke cigarettes also decreased slightly in 1997. In 1994 and 1995, there were more than 142,000 cocaine-related emergency-room episodes per year, the highest number ever reported since these events were tracked starting in 1978. Illegal drugs present a serious threat to Americans who use these drugs. Addiction is a chronic, relapsing disease that changes the chemistry of the brain in harmful ways. The abuse of inhalants and solvents found in legal products like hair spray, paint thinner, and industrial cleaners—called "huffing" (through the mouth) or "sniffing" (through the nose)—has come to public attention in recent years. *The National Household Survey on Drug Abuse* discovered that among youngsters ages 12 to 17, this dangerous practice doubled between 1991 and 1996 from 10.3 percent to 21 percent. An alarming large number of children died the very first time they tried inhalants, which can also cause brain damage or injure other vital organs.

Another threat to public health comes from firearm injuries. Fortunately, the number of such assaults declined between 1993 and 1996. Nevertheless, excessive violence in our culture—as depicted in the mass media—may have contributed to the random shootings at Columbine High School in Littleton, Colorado, and elsewhere. The government and private citizens are rethinking how to reduce the fascination with violence so that America can become a safer, healthier place to live.

The "smart money" is on improving health care for everyone. Only recently did we realize that the gap between the "haves" and "have-nots" had a significant health component. One more reason to invest in education is that schooling produces better health.

In 1835, Alexis de Tocqueville, a French visitor to America, wrote, "In America, the passion for physical well-being is general." Today, as then, health and fitness are front-page items. But with the greater scientific and technological resources now available to us, we are in a far stronger position to make good health care available to everyone. With the greater technological threats to us as we approach the 21st century, the need to do so is more urgent than ever before. Comprehensive information about basic biology, preventative medicine, medical and surgical treatments, and related ethical and public policy issues can help you arm yourself with adequate knowledge to be healthy throughout life.

FOREWORD

Sandra Thurman, Director, Office of National AIDS Policy, The White House

A hundred years ago, an era was marked by discovery, invention, and the infinite possibilities of progress. Nothing piqued society's curiosity more than the mysterious workings of the human body. They poked and prodded, experimented with new remedies and discarded old ones, increased longevity and reduced death rates. But not even the most enterprising minds of the day could have dreamed of the advancements that would soon become our shared reality. Could they have envisioned that we would vaccinate millions of children against polio? Ward off the annoyance of allergy season with a single pill? Or give life to a heart that had stopped keeping time?

As we stand on the brink of a new millennium, the progress made during the last hundred years is indeed staggering. And we continue to push forward every minute of every day. We now exist in a working global community, blasting through cyber-space at the speed of light, sharing knowledge and up-to-the-minute technology. We are in a unique position to benefit from the world's rich fabric of traditional healing practices while continuing to explore advances in modern medicine. In the halls of our medical schools, tomorrow's healers are learning to appreciate the complexities of our whole person. We are not only keeping people alive, we are keeping them well.

Although we deserve to rejoice in our progress, we must also remember that our health remains a complex web. Our world changes with each step forward and we are continuously faced with new threats to our well-being. The air we breathe has become polluted, the water tainted, and new killers have emerged to challenge us in ways we are just beginning to understand. AIDS, in particular, continues to tighten its grip on America's most fragile communities, and place our next generation in jeopardy.

Facing these new challenges will require us to find inventive ways to stay healthy. We already know the dangers of alcohol, smoking and drug abuse. We also understand the benefits of early detection for illnesses like cancer and heart disease, two areas where scientists have made significant in-roads to treatment. We have become a well-informed society, and with that information comes a renewed emphasis on preventative care and a sense of personal responsibility to care for both ourselves and those who need our help.

Read. Re-read. Study. Explore the amazing working machine that is the human body. Share with your friends and your families what you have learned. It is up to all of us living together as a community to care for our well-being, and to continue working for a healthier quality of life.

1

WHY LEARN ABOUT REPRODUCTION?

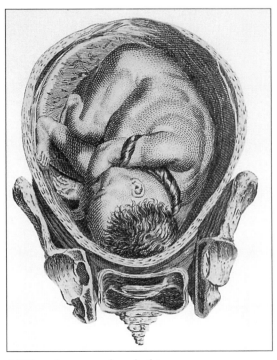

A 16th-century engraving of a fetus

Each of the more than 5 billion people on earth, as well as every person who ever lived, began life as a single cell smaller than a tiny dot. Try to imagine the remarkable process that can change 1 barely visible cell into more than 200 million highly specialized cells in just 9 months. Think of the intricate series of events that can transform a single fertilized egg into a fully developed baby that weighs 6 billion times more than the tiny dot from which it grew.

For most people, the time during which a baby forms is curtained in mystery. It is hard to imagine that after only 40 days into its 9 months of growth, a developing embryo can have a heart that already has been beating for 2 weeks and a brain and nervous system capable of sending out impulses. It is even more difficult to imagine that this minute human is still so small that it can fit easily into a walnut shell. Picturing such a miniature "person" and understanding that it has all of its vital organs, yet weighs no more than an ordinary book of matches, gives one a glimpse into the remarkable nature of human reproduction.

The reproductive system is unique. Unlike other bodily systems, it does nothing to keep an animal alive in any way. Yet, it probably is nature's most vital system. It is the reproductive system alone that determines whether or not any species will continue to exist. If any group of living things does not reproduce, the species dies out forever. It might be argued, then, that nature designed all the other body systems just to make certain that the reproductive system can do its job.

ASEXUAL REPRODUCTION

The job of the reproductive system is to create a younger living creature from a part of an older one. Simple, single-celled organisms reproduce all by themselves. During *asexual reproduction,* or one-parent reproduction, an organism simply splits itself into two or more new beings. One such splitting process is called fission. It produces two exact replicas of the parent. Other asexual processes include budding and the generation of spores. These produce more than two new organisms. In all cases, a special substance called *deoxyribonucleic acid* (DNA) is passed on to each offspring. This DNA carries coded information that determines the organism's characteristics. It guarantees that the new organisms will be the same as the parent from which they are formed. The offspring continue the reproductive process during their own life cycle, as do all the identical generations that follow.

Surprisingly, some simple organisms are able to reproduce both asexually and sexually. The volvox is a tiny creature that lives in large clusters, or colonies, in freshwater ponds. During the spring and summer the volvox divides itself over and over to make new colonies. Some of the colonies are male, and some are female. During the fall and winter, male and female colonies join together to reproduce sexually.

Plants have developed a unique form of reproduction that works both sexually and asexually. Most plants have a complete set of male

Bristle-footed worms, such as the one shown here on coral, reproduce asexually. Mature worms are equipped to be both male and female and so do not need a partner to reproduce. This ability enables the species to survive at times when mates—if they were actually needed—would be hard to find.

and female reproductive organs. Insects and birds spread reproductive material from one plant to another, but if this does not occur a single plant can become both mother and father to its baby plants. Bristle-footed worms also are fully equipped to be both the male and female parents to their young. Some sea worms, such as clam worms, become males during one season and change into females during another. Even more fascinating is the slipper limpet, which changes its sex in response to the sex of the other limpets that come its way. If the newcomer is male, the limpet becomes female. If a newcomer is female, the limpet turns into a male. Whatever the problem, each species has a way of surmounting the many obstacles to reproducing itself.

SEXUAL REPRODUCTION

During *sexual reproduction,* DNA is passed on from two different parents, one male and one female. The offspring will inherit some characteristics from each of the parents. In this way, as different combinations of characteristics are inherited, nature provides for greater variety among somewhat similar living things. Variety increases the chances that some individuals will have characteristics that better help them to survive in a changing environment. At the same time, nature is careful to preserve the identity of each of its many distinct creatures. For example, tigers cannot mate with giraffes. Among all living things, only members of the same species can mate and produce offspring capable of reproducing.

Sexual reproduction has many variations. Female birds and reptiles lay eggs that have been fertilized by the male. The offspring develop outside of the mother inside the egg. Marsupials, such as kangaroos, give birth to offspring not fully mature. These babies finish the development process in the mother's pouch. Dogs, cats, monkeys, and other more highly developed animals give birth to a fully formed baby as humans do. Although sexual reproduction varies among species, there are basic similarities in mechanism and development.

This book looks at the way in which human beings reproduce. Humans are capable of forming complicated thoughts and making deci-

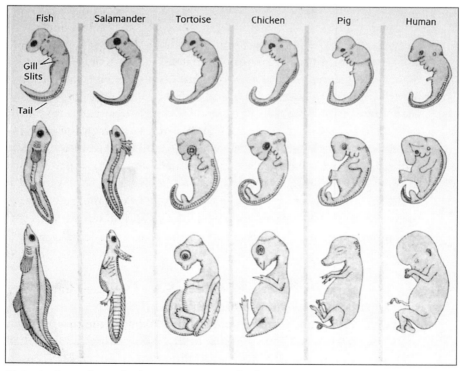

Methods of sexual reproduction vary among species, but as this diagram comparing vertebrate embryos shows, there are great similarities in embryonic development, especially at early stages.

sions based on knowledge and experience. In this respect the human reproductive system is special. It is the only body system that people can control by conscious choice. It can be kept waiting until a person is ready to have children and it is the only system that a perfectly healthy person may decide never to use to its full extent. However, the choices that people make about their own reproductive system are often directly related to how well they understand how this system works.

Today, men and women can choose when and if they want to become parents. They can plan the number of children they want in their family. They even have a variety of options about having babies if their own reproductive system breaks down. It is important to understand that men and women are faced with many decisions about reproduction long before a baby is ever born.

The reproductive system is also unique because it cannot function without the active cooperation of another person. Males and females must unite in the act of sexual intercourse to naturally produce offspring. But sexual intercourse is not only an act of reproduction. It is an act by which people share a loving, intimate experience. It is one way in which people express their affection for one another. It is part of a personal relationship they share in a special way. As a result, many people have sexual intercourse throughout their adult life, even when they do not want to have children.

However, any act of sexual intercourse between a man and a woman can normally result in a pregnancy. Babies, even if they are not planned, need parents who can provide them with a good home and with responsible care. Today, more and more teenagers are having sexual relationships, and more and more teenagers are having babies. According to the U.S. Department of Health and Human Services, there are over 30,000 pregnancies each year among girls under 15; 500,000 American teenagers have abortions every year; 5 out of 10 teenage females who have a child before age 17 will be pregnant again before age 20; and 4 out of every 100 girls ages 15 to 17 has had a baby. In the United States, every year approximately a million teenage girls become pregnant. This is the highest rate of any industrialized nation in the world.

Babies of such young mothers are twice as likely to die in infancy as those born to women in their twenties. These babies are much more likely to be born premature or with a low birth weight. Teenagers have more medically complicated pregnancies. Teenagers are also largely unprepared for the physical, emotional, and financial burdens of parenting.

A Snapshot Profile of 15- to 19-Year-Old Teenage Women in 1997: Sexual Activity, Pregnancy, Childbearing, and Related Behaviors

In 1997, there were almost 9½ million 15- to 19-year-old teenage girls. Among them, approximately

9 million had never been married

Never Married 95%

Ever Married 5%

5.7 million were sexually active, 3.6 million of whom had never been married

| **Sexually Active 60%** | **Not Sexually Active 40%** |

Never Married 55%   Ever Married 5%

5.2 million used some method of contraception,
4.9 million of whom had never been married

| **Contraception Used 55%** | **No Contraception Used 45%** |

Never Married 52%   Ever Married 3%   Sexually Active 5%   Not Sexually Active 40%

1 million became pregnant, 900,000 of whom were not married

| Pregnant 11% | **Not Pregnant 89%** |

Married 2%
Unmarried 9%   Sexually Active, No Contraception 4%   Sexually Active, Effective Contraception 45%   Not Sexually Active 40%

500,000 gave birth, 385,800 as unmarried mothers

| Births 5% | **No Births 95%** |

Miscarriages 1%
Abortions 5%
Married 2%
Unmarried 3%   Sexually Active, Not Pregnant 49%   Not Sexually Active 40%

110,000 had already given birth at least once

No Repeat Births 99%

Repeat Births 1%

Source: U.S. Dept. of Health and Human Services

Teenage pregnancy is a major problem in the United States. Every year, approximately 1 million teenage girls become pregnant and 500,000 give birth. Increased availability of information and contraceptives could help to significantly decrease these numbers.

Many teenage mothers did not know enough about reproduction to have prevented their own pregnancies. Young people who are unaware of their own reproductive processes have a good chance of becoming adults who are equally unaware. A person who does not understand reproduction is unable to make intelligent and informed choices about his or her own sexual activity and about having or not having children.

On the other side of this problem are a large number of people whose reproductive systems are not creating the babies that they want. Of couples trying to have a baby, 10% to 15% suffer from *infertility,* the inability to have a child, which has many causes. Not being able to become a parent may be distressing. But not knowing how to deal with infertility can be even more distressing.

Often, people feel that they are in some way inadequate if they cannot become a parent. Things go wrong with the reproductive system just as they do with other body systems. Anyone who understands its causes will more easily view infertility as a setback in a body system, rather than as a personal failure.

The importance of understanding the reproductive system goes far beyond the area of family planning. Every organ of the human body is made of living tissue that is susceptible to a wide variety of disorders. The organs of the reproductive system are no exception. In fact, every year, thousands of Americans die because diseases of these organs are undetected and untreated for too long.

According to the American Cancer Society, 175,000 females and 1,300 males in the United States were diagnosed as having breast cancer in 1999. In the same year, about 14,500 women died of ovarian cancer and 11,200 died of uterine cancer. Also, each year, nearly 1,400 men are diagnosed as having testicular cancer. That many cancers have a high cure rate if detected and treated early makes these statistics even more distressing.

Reproductive organs are also sexual organs, and these organs are the means by which a group of serious diseases are transmitted from person to person through sexual contact. According to the U.S. Centers for Disease Control (CDC), more than 8 million new cases of *sexually transmitted diseases* (STDs) are reported every year. More than a million of these cases develop in teenagers. And these numbers do not include cases of *acquired immune deficiency syndrome* (AIDS), a fatal disease of the body's immune system that can be spread by sexual contact.

Having the right information can minimize the chances of contracting an STD or spreading it to someone else. Learning how to reduce the risks of infection and knowing when to seek treatment are the best lines of defense against these highly contagious and sometimes incurable diseases.

Despite their problems, the reproductive systems of males and females are as remarkable as they are complicated. By becoming aware of the reproductive system, people will be better prepared to make the important choices that affect their life and the lives of their children for years to come.

2

THE STUDY OF REPRODUCTION AND GENETICS

Aristotle (left), from Dictionnaire Raisonne Universel d'Histoire Naturelle, *1775*

Humans have always reproduced, continuing the species, but initially they were moved by instinct rather than by an understanding of the process. People wondered how new, small creatures—their children—were formed. The processes by which new life is created from old were not known. People also wondered how it was that children resembled their parents, their grandparents, and their siblings. Sometimes the resemblance was close, sometimes there was little resemblance at all, and sometimes similarities might skip a generation, appearing in a grandparent and a child but not in a parent. These questions were to be answered gradually at first, over a period of centuries, and then in amazingly quick succession, in the latter half of the 20th century. The story of these answers is the history of the sciences of reproduction and genetics.

REPRODUCTION

In ancient times, many people believed that spiritual forces controlled all the rhythmic cycles of the universe. Not only did these forces bring about the regular reappearance of the sun and the moon and the consistent return of the seasons year after year, but they also were thought to be responsible for the life cycle of birth, growth, and death. Philosophers, religious thinkers, scientists, and doctors pondered and argued over these phenomena for ages. They built upon or extrapolated from the discoveries and ideas of those before them, and slowly the mystery unfolded.

Ancient Times

Aristotle, the ancient Greek philosopher (384–322 B.C.), observed the development of a chick embryo more than 2,000 years ago. He believed that some supernatural spirit brought form and shape to everything in nature. In *Generation of Animals,* he claimed that male semen was guided by spiritual forces to bring forth limbs and organs from female menstrual blood. In other words, the substance of the embryo came from the female, but the stimulus for growth came from the male, embodying the soul or spirit of the universe. Aristotle also imagined that all parts of the developing fetus appeared and became identifiable at the same time.

Five hundred years after Aristotle, the Greek physician Galen (A.D. 129–199) added his own ideas. He believed that a miniature, preformed embryo existed in the womb of the female. He thought that contact with the male permitted the tiny embryo to break out of its "shell" and begin to grow. Galen even believed that every female baby contained another preformed baby and that each baby was stuffed inside another all through the generations.

This theory became known as *emboîtement,* which means encasement, or capsulization.

In the ancient world, reproduction was believed to be caused by metaphysical, or spiritual, forces and so was not a field to be investigated by science. One of the only physicians to show an interest in the birth process was Soranus of Ephesus, who lived in Rome in the 2nd century A.D. Soranus was the first known *gynecologist,* or specialist in women's reproductive organs. He assisted women who were having difficulty in delivering their babies, and he perfected a way of turning a baby to a headfirst position. But Soranus was the last such specialist for a long time. His writings dominated the field for 15 centuries. Scientific work related to reproduction virtually disappeared in Europe during the medieval period.

During this period, most people accepted the teachings of Aristotle, Galen, and Soranus. Pregnancy and childbirth were the "burden" of women and *menstruation* their "curse." Hebrew tradition considered a menstruating woman to be unclean. During the time of her menstruation, or period, she could not be touched by a man, lest he be contaminated by her impurity. Muslim culture prohibited any male, even a doctor, from examining a woman's genital organs.

For hundreds of years, childbearing was solely a woman's concern. Pregnant women were advised and attended at home by *midwives.* These women, who were trained to deliver babies and care for new mothers, were the obstetricians of their time. To this day, the midwife remains an important figure in the field of childbirth.

Renaissance

After centuries of inactivity, new advances were made in 1513, in the city of Worms, Germany. It was here that Eucharius Rösslin wrote a small book entitled *Rosengarten*—the first textbook ever written about *obstetrics,* or child delivery. And 30 years later, at the medical school at Padua, Italy, the female reproductive system began to receive serious study.

There, in 1543, anatomy professor Andreas Vesalius published *De humani corporis fabrica.* This book contained the first accurate descriptions ever made of female internal organs. Not long after, Bartolommeo Eustachio, a student of Vesalius's, correctly drew a *uterus* for a series of anatomical plates. Unfortunately, these drawings were stored in the Vatican and not found again for another 150 years.

Gabriello Fallopio succeeded Vesalius in his post at Padua. Fallopio accurately described more of the female system: the *vagina,* the *placenta,* the *ovaries,* and what were later to become known as the *fallopian tubes.* These 16th-century physicians opened the door to a renewed interest in *gynecology,* or the study of women's reproductive organs.

A 16th-century illustration from Eucharius Rösslins's book on midwives shows a midwife delivering the baby of a woman (sitting on birthstool). For centuries, midwives, not doctors, delivered babies and cared for pregnant women.

Modern Times

William Harvey was an English physician who had studied at Padua. In 1602, Harvey opened a medical practice in England, continuing to study the human body. Through his innovative experiments, Harvey gave the medical world its first true understanding of how blood travels in the body.

Harvey did not fully agree with Aristotle's ideas on reproduction. Harvey believed that the egg was the more powerful force. To Harvey, the semen simply stimulated the embryo to develop. Such guesswork, even among trained men of medicine, prevailed until nearly the end of the 17th century, when the first glimpse of truth emerged with the invention of the microscope.

The compound, or two-lens, microscope had been invented in 1590 by two Dutch lens makers, Jans and Zacharias Janssen. However, it was not until 1665 that Robert Hooke, an English scientist, used the microscope to make some very important observations. When Hooke looked closely at a thin slice of cork, he realized with amazement that it is made up of tiny hollow chambers, which he called *cells* (from the Latin word *cella,* meaning "little room"). Hooke's observations electrified the scientific world.

In 1667, a Dutch shopkeeper, Antonie van Leeuwenhoek, began to peer through his own homemade microscope at a world too small to be seen by the naked eye. Leeuwenhoek was neither a scientist nor a doctor. He was a draper in the city of Delft, who ground fine lenses in his spare time. Through some of his hundreds of lenses, Leeuwenhoek saw tiny creatures on bits of slime mold and in drops of rainwater. In one of his experiments, Leeuwenhoek examined a drop of seminal fluid under a lens. There he saw what no one had ever seen before—a living sperm cell.

For nearly a hundred years, controversy over the reproduction process continued. One group of scientists were *ovists.* They insisted that a preformed baby existed in the ovary of the mother. Another group, called *homunculists,* argued that the new baby was fully formed on the head of the father's sperm. They viewed the womb only as an incubator in which the preformed spermbaby could grow.

In 1759, a German anatomist challenged the theories of both of these groups. In that year, Caspar Friedrich Wolff published his *Theoria generationis* after studying chick embryos under a microscope. Wolff rejected the idea of a preformed baby. He believed that both parents contribute to the formation of a developing embryo.

Wolff came to this conclusion without ever having seen a true egg cell. It was another 68 years before an Estonian naturalist, Karl Ernst von Baer, discovered the mammalian egg. In 1827, Baer examined the ovary of a dog. In *De ovi mammalium et hominis genesi,* he described "a yellowish-white point" that he thought was so clearly an *ovule,* or immature egg, under the microscope "that a blind man could hardly deny it."

After this, the science of *embryology,* the study of the formation and development of organisms, developed. In 1838, two German scientists, Matthias J. Schleiden and Theodor Schwann, presented a revolutionary theory. Taking Hooke's theories even further, they stated that cells are the basic units that make up *all* living things. They said that these living cells divide to form other cells. In 1858, Rudolf Virchow, a German pathologist, established that all cells come from other preexisting cells. The *cell theory* led the way toward a more realistic understanding of reproduction.

The 19th century also saw great changes in the field of gynecology. Women were still thought of as prisoners of their reproductive system. For many doctors, the uterus was the focus of attention. They believed that the uterus caused women to be weak, nervous, and chronically ill. In 1850, Dr. William A. Alcott of Boston wrote that half of America's women suffered from headaches and nervousness that stemmed from disorders of the uterus. In fact, many doctors believed that the uterus was the cause of most of the physical and emotional problems that women experienced.

The treatments that were commonplace between 1830 and 1860 for problems of the uterus would evoke horror today. For example, a *prolapsed,* or dropped, uterus would be pushed back into place by hand. The treatment for infections of the uterus ranged from the use of leeches to *cauterizing,* or burning, the patient with powerful astringents such as silver nitrate. Very resistant infections might be treated with a white-hot iron. It was not unusual to repeat this treatment several times. It was excruciatingly painful and probably killed more women than it cured. Fortunately, by the 1880s doctors understood a great deal more about germs and eliminated the treatment.

In 1845, James Marion Sims, a Philadelphia physician, attended a woman who had a displaced uterus. After examining the patient, Sims did something unusual. He placed her in a lateral position, on her side, making it much easier to manipulate and view the uterus. This position became known as *Sims' position.*

Sims also made a number of important contributions to gynecological surgery. He invented a special, curved *speculum.* This instrument made the patient more comfortable as the walls of the vagina were pushed back to give a clearer view of the internal organs. Sims also developed a silver suture to close surgical cuts with less danger of infection. Sims was also the first doctor to use a *catheter,* or thin tube, to empty a woman's bladder.

It took four years of experimentation for Sims to perfect this catheter technique. He could not have done it without 3 black slave women, known only as Anarcha, Betsy, and Lucy, who submitted to as many as 30 attempts each to penetrate their bladder. In 1855, Sims opened Women's Hospital, which became a major gynecological center for the treatment of reproductive organ disorders.

The 1800s marked the end of centuries of unsanitary conditions in hospitals. Hospitals in the early part of the century rarely had running water, and what they did have was often contaminated. Surgeons wiped their instruments on their trousers, and bed linens were rarely changed. Hospital infections were rampant, and up to one-third of all women giving birth died of *puerperal,* or childbed, fever, a form of blood poisoning.

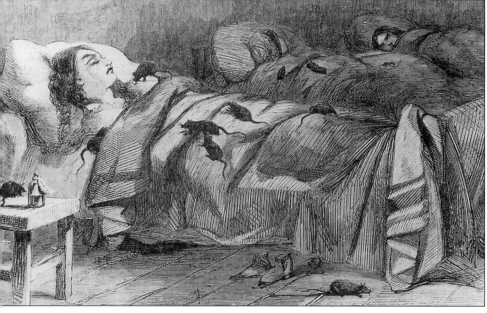

An 1860 depiction of a sick woman in New York City's Bellevue Hospital. Until the early 19th century, doctors understood little about germs or the spread of disease.

A major advance was made by Ignaz Semmelweis, a Hungarian-born doctor who worked at a hospital in Vienna. In 1846, he observed two different maternity wards. One ward was attended by medical students right after they finished dissecting corpses in an anatomy class. In that ward one out of every eight women died of puerperal fever. The second ward, attended by midwives with no such contamination, showed a much lower death rate. Semmelweis ordered all attendants in both wards to wash their hands. A year later, the death rate had dropped to zero. Despite this success, it took many years for hospital authorities to accept Semmelweis's ideas. The pioneering physician returned to his native Budapest, where he was made professor of obstetrics and given the freedom to practice his clean methods in his own ward.

In the United States, a similar plea was put forth by Oliver Wendell Holmes, Sr., a philosopher and physician. In 1843, Holmes published a paper entitled "Contagiousness of Puerperal Fever." It was largely ignored until 1847, and not until the end of the century did doctors fully understand and accept the connection between dirt and hospital deaths. *Bacteria* (unicellular organisms) and *viruses* (minute acellular parasites) cannot be seen by the naked eye but cause disease and infections of all sorts.

By the end of the 19th century, more powerful microscopes allowed scientists to see the process of fertilization. They were able to observe the actual union of a sperm cell and an egg cell. It became clear that both parents contributed something to the embryo. Still, no one understood just how the parent cells were instructed to share their identities with their offspring.

Advances in gynecological surgery also continued. In 1909, Ephraim McDowell removed the ovary of a 47-year-old woman in Danville, Kentucky. This was the first *ovariectomy* ever performed; it was done before anesthesia was invented and before antiseptic surgery was understood. McDowell's patient survived another 31 years. The surgery itself became a common operation by the mid-20th century.

GENETICS

Once it became clear that a sperm cell from a man joined with an egg cell, or *ovum,* from a woman to form what would develop into a baby, the major area of investigation shifted to the field of genetics. What was contained in the sperm and ovum that carried hereditary information, and how was this information translated into the characteristics of a person?

Chromosomes

Discoveries in the late 1800s began to answer many questions. German biologist Walther Flemming stained cells and examined the dark center area—the *nucleus*—that every cell had. It seemed to play an important part in the cell-division process. He called the dye-absorbing material in the nucleus *chromatin* after the Greek word for "color." Flemming observed the cell as it divided in two and noted that the chromatin drew up into threadlike structures, later named *chromosomes,* Greek for "colored bodies."

When a cell divides, the chromosomes split lengthwise, held together in the middle by a *centromere.* The chromosomes then line up along the middle of the cell; they pull apart, dividing through the centromere. Each set of newly divided chromosomes migrates to an opposite side of the cell. This division of the nucleus is known as *mitosis.* Next, the body of the cell divides, and, finally, new *cell membranes* (in animals) or *cell walls* (in plants) form, completing the creation of two identical *daughter cells.*

Although they believed that most cells reproduce by mitosis, 19th-century scientists felt that there must be a different process for the formation of sex cells, the sperm and egg. If sex cells, or *gametes,* were formed this way then they would contain the same number of chromosomes as the parent cell. When they joined to form an embryo they would have double this number. German biologist August Weismann hypothesized that another process formed gametes. In this process, now known as *meiosis,* each new sex cell would have only half the number of chromosomes as the parent cell. This theory was proven by a Belgian scientist, Edouard van Beneden.

This new knowledge sparked more research in genetics. About 1900, the work of an obscure monk, done almost 40 years before, was rediscovered and became the groundwork for all the discoveries to follow.

Mendel's Experiments

In the 1860s, Gregor Mendel conducted a series of plant-breeding experiments in the garden of his monastery. Mendel worked with pea plants that showed different characteristics: short stems or long stems, purple flowers or white flowers, smooth seeds or wrinkled seeds. By *pollinating,* or joining the male reproductive cells of one plant to the female reproductive cells of another, Mendel was able to observe those traits that were passed from the parent plants to the new pea plants. Mendel started his work with plants that bred *true,* or showed a certain trait for several generations. He then *crossed,* or mated, plants with contrasting traits. After crossing a variety of contrasting plants, Mendel planted the resulting seeds and recorded what happened to them. They were *hybrids,* or offspring of true parents with different traits. He then planted the seeds of new hybrid plants and recorded these results. From these experiments, Mendel drew his conclusions.

Whenever Mendel crossed plants that were true for a specific trait with plants that were true for a contrasting trait, only one of the traits showed up in the offspring. For example, a cross of true tall plants and true short plants always produced tall offspring. Mendel realized that in each pair of contrasting traits, one was stronger than the other. Mendel observed that tallness in pea plants was a strong, or *dominant* trait. Shortness was a weak, or *recessive* trait. When combined, the dominant trait always showed up and the recessive trait remained hidden.

Mendel continued to experiment with the hybrid offspring he had produced. He allowed these plants to *self-pollinate,* or fertilize themselves. In the offspring of the hybrids, three out of every four plants showed dominant traits. The other one showed recessive traits. This proved true time after time and with various traits. These traits always showed up in a definite ratio: 75% to 25%.

By plotting the patterns of his findings, Mendel concluded that each trait passed on to the next generation was made up of two *factors,* as he called them. A true tall plant had two factors for tallness. A hybrid tall plant had one factor for tallness and one for shortness, but, because tallness is dominant, the plant was tall. Only when both factors called for shortness, and no dominant factor for tallness was present, he hypothesized, did shortness actually become a characteristic of the plant. Mendel did not understand what these factors were. Mendel published his findings in 1865, but, when he died in 1884, they still remained unknown to the world of science.

Since Mendel's time, much has been discovered, and later experiments have altered and expanded on his findings. Factors are not always completely dominant or recessive; some traits have more than two factors, and these factors are now called *genes.* But much of Mendel's work has stood the test of time, and he is remembered as one of the founders of the field of genetics.

Genetic Information

The rediscovery of Mendel's experiments marked the beginning of a string of discoveries that were to radically change the way people thought about life. In the early 1900s, a biologist named Thomas Hunt Morgan discovered that chromosomes carry the cell's genetic information. This discovery came from the observation of a small fly, *Drosophila melanogaster,* which has eight large chromosomes that are easy to see under a microscope.

In the 1940s, Oswald T. Avery, Colin M. MacLeod, and Maclyn McCarty probed into the chemistry of the chromosome. Their research at the Rockefeller Institute in New York isolated one of the most famous substances in the human body: DNA. They proved that it was the genetic material of the bacteria with which they were working. Others soon proved that DNA was the hereditary material of all living organisms.

People now knew that living matter is made up of cells; most cells have a nucleus; and the nucleus contains chromosomes. Chromosomes contain genes, each of which is the code for a certain trait. And this information is coded into the structure of the DNA *molecule*. A molecule is a combination of atoms making up a substance with different properties from its constituent atoms.

DNA

In the early 1950s, a race began between two groups of researchers to discover the structure of DNA. The top contenders were believed to be a team working at the California Institute of Technology, headed by Linus Pauling and Robert B. Corey, and another team working at Cambridge University in England, led by an American biologist, James D. Watson, and a British physicist, Francis H. C. Crick.

In April 1953, Watson and Crick published their results, and the Cambridge team won the race. They designed a model of the DNA molecule in the form of a *double helix,* or two coils joined through the center like the steps of a spiral staircase. The coils are made of alternating molecules of phosphate and deoxyribose, a sugar. Each step is a pair of linked nitrogen compounds: adenine, guanine, cytosine, and thymine. In 1962, these two scientists joined their fellow researcher, M. H. F. Wilkins, as recipients of the Nobel Prize in physiology or medicine, along with M. F. Perutz and J. C. Kendrew, who won in chemistry, for their work with DNA. Another researcher on the project, Rosalind Franklin, died before her contribution could be acknowledged by the Nobel committee.

The number of chromosomes in a human cell was unknown until 1956, when J. H. Tijo and Albert Levan reported from Sweden that the correct count was 46. How the *coding,* or the arrangement of nitrogen compounds within DNA, worked was not understood until the early 1960s. Scientists then discovered that the code is based on sequences of three nitrogen compounds. Each gene is made of hundreds of sequences, and each chromosome contains thousands of genes. This explains how 46 chromosomes can encode every trait in the human body.

Understanding DNA led to the development, in the 1970s, of a new field: *genetic engineering.* Scientists learned to cut and recombine chromosomes at certain locations, creating recombinant DNA. In fewer than three decades, scientists had leaped from the discovery of the molecule to the ability to manipulate it. Genetic engineering holds the potential to cure many genetic disorders. There is also the possibility of

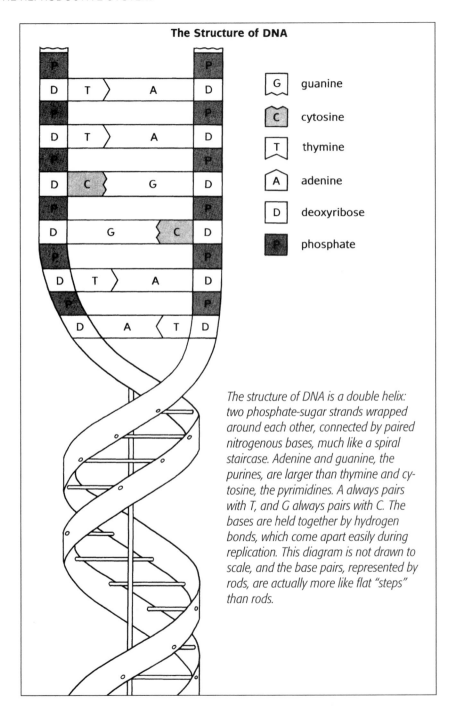

The Structure of DNA

G — guanine
C — cytosine
T — thymine
A — adenine
D — deoxyribose
P — phosphate

The structure of DNA is a double helix: two phosphate-sugar strands wrapped around each other, connected by paired nitrogenous bases, much like a spiral staircase. Adenine and guanine, the purines, are larger than thymine and cytosine, the pyrimidines. A always pairs with T, and G always pairs with C. The bases are held together by hydrogen bonds, which come apart easily during replication. This diagram is not drawn to scale, and the base pairs, represented by rods, are actually more like flat "steps" than rods.

choosing and recombining genetic material to custom design a baby. Although genetic engineering is in use now, these more dramatic and controversial applications are still in the future.

In 1989, the National Institutes of Health embarked on the most ambitious study ever attempted in human genetics. With a budget of about $3 billion in public and private funds, scientists launched a 15-year project to map the human genome, to locate every gene and determine what traits it controls. The complete set of instructions in the nucleus is called a genome. With the help of computer experts, biologists, and engineers, geneticists hope to predict more accurately an individual's vulnerability to inherited diseases.

With the knowledge sought by the human genome project and the techniques of genetic engineering, scientists hope to develop a way to alter the instructions in the human genome. If such *gene therapy* becomes a reality, it may one day eliminate genetic defects completely.

Human Inheritance

The human body is made up of about 100 trillion cells. The nucleus of each cell (except red blood cells) contains thousands of genes that carry hereditary information. That means that a nucleus contains a complete blueprint for a man or a woman. There are genes for every inherited trait. For example, there are genes for nose shape, for eye color, for skin color, and even for dimples.

All of the genes in an ordinary cell are linked together like a string of beads on 23 pairs of complementary chromosomes. This means that every nucleus contains 46 chromosomes, arranged in groups of 2. For every gene on one chromosome in any pair, there is a corresponding gene on the other member. The only exception to this exact pairing is a man's pair of sex chromosomes.

If each parent transmitted all 46 chromosomes to his or her offspring, the new baby would end up with 92 chromosomes. In order that offspring do not end up with double the number of chromosomes they need, reproductive cells do not have paired sets. Sperms cells and egg cells carry only 23 single strands of chromosomes. This happens because the chromosome pairs separate before reproductive cells are formed. Half the cells receive one of the pair, and half receive the other.

Therefore, at conception, there are 23 chromosomes in the sperm and 23 in the egg. When the 2 cells unite, forming a *zygote*, it receives all 46. The chromosomes pair up according to the type of information they contain. One chromosome of each pair comes from the egg cell of the mother, and the other chromosome comes from the sperm cell of the father.

Some human traits are inherited in the same way as those of Mendel's pea plants. These include the length of eyelashes and the shape of the hairline. However, most characteristics are transmitted by more than one gene. Skin color, for example, is affected by at least eight different genes. This is why there is such a vast range of skin color. If a trait has a wide range of possibilities, it is not controlled by a single gene.

Two of the chromosomes in the cell nucleus are called the *sex chromosomes.* X chromosomes have many genes and look like other strands of genetic material. Y chromosomes are smaller than others and have a Y shape. Females have two matching X chromosomes. Male sex chromosomes are the only unmatched pair in the cell. All human males have both an X and a Y chromosome in their cells. When a male produces sperm, the XY chromosomes separate. Half the sperm receive X chromosomes, and half receive Y chromosomes. The X and Y chromosomes will determine the sex of a new baby.

Not many people realize that the sex of a baby depends on which type of sperm fertilizes the egg. If a sperm with an X chromosome fertilizes an egg (which always has an X chromosome), the embryo has an XX chromosome pair. It will develop into a female. If a sperm with a Y chromosome fertilizes the egg, the embryo has an XY chromosome pair and will develop into a male.

Some traits are controlled by genes that are on the sex chromosomes. In the early 1900s, in his experiments with *Drosophila,* Thomas Hunt Morgan cross-mated hybrid red-eyed and white-eyed flies and discovered that all of the white-eyed flies were males and all of the red-eyed flies were females. The sex of the offspring had something to do with the inheritance of eye color. The human Y chromosome is smaller than the X. This means that most genes on the X chromosome do not have matching genes on the Y chromosome. Genes that are on the X chromosome but not on the Y (such as *Drosophila's* eye color gene) are called sex-linked genes. Some sex-linked genes play an important part in human heredity.

When a male receives a recessive sex-linked gene, he inherits the trait. This happens because there is no dominant trait on the Y chromosome to hide it. A female who receives a recessive sex-linked trait shows the trait only if she receives two recessive genes. She receives two X chromosomes. One of them may carry a dominant gene to mask the trait. A number of human defects and diseases are transmitted by sex-linked genes. Other disorders are passed on by recessive genes hidden in both parents. Still other genetic diseases are associated with particular ethnic or racial groups.

3

THE MALE
REPRODUCTIVE SYSTEM

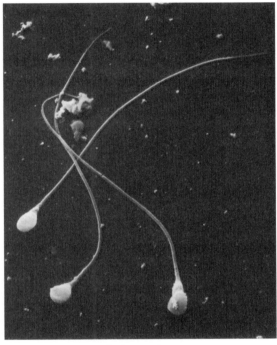

Human sperm magnified 4,000 times

When living things reproduce through sexual reproduction, the male parent must fertilize the female egg cell with *spermatozoa*, or sperm. In most lower organisms, fertilization is an uncomplicated process that ordinarily takes place outside the parents' body. The male frog, for example, deposits his sperm on the eggs of the female frog by releasing them into the lake or pond in which her eggs already have been laid.

In more highly developed animals, the sperm and egg must meet inside the body of the female. Therefore, the male must have some way of putting the sperm inside the female's body. Some fish, such as sharks and rays, expel sperm through *claspers,* extensions of their pelvic fins. Snakes and lizards have *hemipenes,* organs that can be turned inside out, pushed out of their body, and inserted into the female reptile. In humans and other mammals, the *penis* is the organ that is used for the transfer of sperm to the female reproductive tract.

A male baby is born with reproductive organs just as he is born with the organs that operate his other systems. From the beginning of his life, the human male has a penis, *scrotum, testicles, prostate gland,* and *seminal vesicles*—the components of the male reproductive system. However, a human baby is not ready to reproduce at birth. When his body matures, it will be able to produce millions of sperm at one time, and his penis will be capable of being inserted into a female partner. But this maturation will not take place for years after the baby's birth.

THE PENIS

The penis is part of the *genitals,* or external organs, of the male reproductive system. It consists of a body known as the *shaft,* and a sensitive, cap-shaped tip, known as the *glans,* or head. The inside of the penis has many blood vessels and many nerves. Its great number of nerves makes the penis very sensitive to touch, pressure, and temperature.

Internally, the penis is made of three cylinders of spongy tissue. All three cylinders are dotted with small blood vessels and are bound together by a thick covering membrane. The two side-by-side cylinders on the upper side of the penis are called the cavernous bodies, or *corpora cavernosum.* These cylinders form branching tips, the *crura,* that are attached to the bones of the pelvis.

The cylindrical structure on the underside of the penis is known as the spongy body, or *corpus spongiosum.* This spongy cylinder extends under the cavernous cylinders to include the head of the penis. The spongy glans region of the penis contains many more nerve endings than does the shaft, and is particularly sensitive to physical stimulation.

The movable skin that covers the head of the penis is called the foreskin, or *prepuce.* The foreskin can be surgically removed by a minor operation known as *circumcision.* Circumcision among many Jews and

Muslims is performed for religious reasons, and in some countries, it is often routinely done soon after birth to many male babies. The advantages of circumcision are related to cleanliness and health, although doctors in the United States no longer feel it necessary unless parents request it. The glans of a circumcised penis is easier to clean and has been shown to be less prone to inflammation and infection. An uncircumcised male must be careful to keep the penis clear of foul-smelling *smegma,* a cheesy substance of oils, dead skin, and bacteria that may collect under the foreskin. However, so long as the penis is washed daily, an uncircumcised penis poses no particular health problem.

In addition to the glans, the penis has two other very sensitive areas. One is the *coronal ridge,* a rim of tissue that separates the glans from the shaft of the penis. The other is a triangular section on the underside of the penis where the *frenulum,* a thin strip of skin, is attached to the glans.

The *urethra* is a narrow tube that runs right through the center of the spongy body of the penis. At one end, it forms the *urinary opening* (urethral meatus), through which liquid waste, or urine, leaves the body. At its other end, the urethra branches in three separate directions. As it passes upward into the body, the urethra attaches to a small, chestnut-sized gland known as the prostate and continues upward to join the *bladder,* in which urine is stored. Immediately before branching to the bladder, the urethra forms a connection with the seminal vesicles, two small structures that lie near the base of the bladder. The prostate and the seminal vesicles produce important fluids in which sperm travel.

The spongy tissues of the penis are interlaced with many large blood vessels. These vessels supply the penis with a constant, even flow of blood. Most of the time, the penis is flaccid, or relaxed. However, if the penis is to be inserted into a female partner, it must become both longer and more rigid. Nature has made this possible by allowing the penis to change from soft to hard material in just a few seconds. When a male becomes sexually aroused, the flow of blood to the penis increases greatly, and the crisscrossing blood vessels expand. Special valves in the vessels keep the blood under pressure, causing the spongy walls of the penis to expand and become hard. This hardening is called an *erection.*

When the human penis is erect, the spongy body on the underside looks and feels like a straight ridge. An erect penis has an average length of 16 centimeters (6¼ inches), with an average diameter at its base of 4 centimeters (1½ inches). In its enlarged and distended state, the penis will be able to channel the sperm it receives from the testicles.

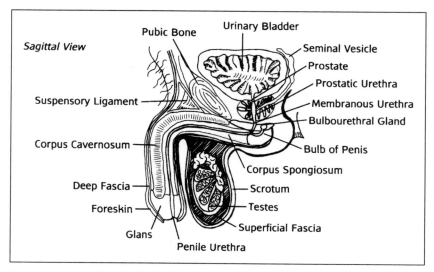

Sagittal View

Pubic Bone
Urinary Bladder
Seminal Vesicle
Prostate
Prostatic Urethra
Suspensory Ligament
Membranous Urethra
Bulbourethral Gland
Corpus Cavernosum
Bulb of Penis
Corpus Spongiosum
Deep Fascia
Scrotum
Foreskin
Testes
Superficial Fascia
Glans
Penile Urethra

Diagram of the male reproductive system

THE TESTES

The testicles, or testes, are the male *gonads,* or organs of sex-cell production. In human fetuses, these two glands develop inside the body, near the kidneys. By the time a boy is born, the testes have moved downward into a pair of pouches known as the scrotum, or scrotal sacs. The scrotum hangs under the penis, and one testicle usually hangs somewhat lower than the other. Both testes are about the same size, in adult males averaging 5 centimeters (2 inches) long, and less than 2.5 centimeters (1 inch) thick, and are highly sensitive to touch or pressure.

The testes have 2 important jobs, both of which normally begin somewhere between the ages of 10 and 12. This is the period of *puberty,* when the body begins to prepare for reproduction. At this time, the *hypothalamus, pituitary gland,* and *pineal glands* trigger special *Leydig's cells* in the testes to produce *testosterone,* a *hormone,* one of a group of substances that regulate growth and function. Testosterone controls male sexual development, causing a number of important changes when boys reach puberty. Among other things, this hormone causes the penis, the testes, and the prostate gland to become larger. It stimulates the growth of pubic and underarm hair and brings about the deepening of the male voice.

The second function of the testes is to manufacture sperm. At the onset of puberty, sperm develop in a series of tightly coiled, microscopic tubes called *seminiferous tubules.* If unrolled, these tiny chambers would measure more than a quarter of a mile in length. In their position in the scrotum, the testes are cooler than the rest of the body, providing the best conditions for producing a high number of sperm.

The testes produce sperm continuously, taking about 46 days to produce each new cell. A human male produces several hundred million sperm each day and many billions of sperm each year. After puberty, men produce sperm for the rest of their life. As they age, the number of sperm decreases, but the testes continue their work to some degree throughout life.

Sperm cells, like egg cells, are produced through meiosis, called *gametogenesis* when sex cells, or gametes, are being created. Thus, each sperm cell has 23 chromosomes, containing genes from the potential father. To create an embryo, the sperm must first reach and fertilize the egg.

THE SPERM

Sperm cells are very tiny, only about one two hundred thousandth the size of an ovum. To imagine their length, consider that almost 5,000 sperm end to end would fit in 1 inch of space. Each cell resembles a small tadpole—with a head, a midpiece, and a long, thin tail, or *flagellum.* The cell nucleus containing DNA is in the head. The tail, which is 12 times longer than the rest of the sperm, lashes back and forth and provides mobility.

When they are first formed, sperm do not use their tails for movement. They are slowly pushed along by other sperm until they reach a long, tightly coiled canal that is folded over the back surface of each testicle. This network of tubing, called the *epididymis,* would be almost 20 feet in length if stretched out.

For several weeks, during which they fully mature, the sperm continue to travel through the tubing. Eventually, they are able to propel themselves forward by rapid tail movements and move into a shorter continuation of the epididymis, the *vas deferens.* These tubes leave the right and left scrotum and curve along the back of the bladder.

From here, the sperm move to the seminal vesicles, two small pouches near the prostate gland. The seminal vesicles join with the ends of the vas deferens to form the *ejaculatory ducts,* where sperm can be stored for several weeks. After this amount of time, sperm that are not *ejaculated,* or transferred out of the body through the penis, will degenerate and die. These cells are reabsorbed into the body and disposed of.

When sperm are ejaculated from the penis, they are carried by liquids secreted by glands along their path. Together, the sperm and the liquid form *semen,* or seminal fluid. The semen transports the sperm through the ejaculatory duct, down through the urethra, and out through an opening at the head of the penis.

About 70% of semen is a yellowish fluid that comes from the seminal vesicles. Another 30% comes from the prostate gland, which adds a thin, clear fluid to the mixture. Other secretions come from two tiny glands on either side of the urethra, the *bulbourethral glands,* sometimes called Cowper's glands, which produce a clear, sticky liquid that is thought to coat the urethra just before the sperm pass through.

Seminal fluid is made up of water, mucus, and a variety of chemicals. Sugar is also present, and acts as an energy source for the sperm. Sperm cannot live in acids, so bases in the semen neutralize the acids from residual urine. *Prostaglandins* in semen are hormones that affect muscles in the female system. The resulting contractions will help the sperm to move upward toward the egg.

When a male is sexually aroused, he may ejaculate his seminal fluid in a series of throbbing spurts. The total volume of semen that is ejaculated usually amounts to about one teaspoonful. But in this small amount of liquid there may be between 200 million and 400 million sperm cells. Most of the sperm will have a very short life, surviving from 1 hour to 48 hours at most. But if only one of these cells reaches its destination and succeeds in entering the female egg, a new life will begin.

DISORDERS OF THE MALE REPRODUCTIVE SYSTEM

Like any part of the body, the components of the male reproductive system are susceptible to certain diseases and problems. It is important to understand the disorders that may occur so that early medical attention can be sought.

Disorders of the Penis

Balanoposthitis   The head of the penis can become irritated and inflamed by infection by various bacteria or *fungi* (simple plantlike, multicellular organisms) or by contact with chemicals in clothing. Men with *diabetes mellitus,* a disease in which individuals cannot break down the sugar in their body, are especially susceptible to *balanoposthitis,* as are uncircumcised men. To treat it, doctors prescribe antibiotics and recommend careful cleaning of the infected area.

Paraphimosis   The foreskin of uncircumcised men can retract behind the head of the penis and then fail to come forward again. This condition, called *paraphimosis,* requires immediate medical attention because the resulting swelling must be treated. Emergency circumcision, total or partial, is the usual treatment.

Priapism   A serious condition that results in prolonged erection, not accompanied by sexual desire, is known as *priapism.* It is rare but painful and may be caused by certain drugs or blood abnormalities. The erection is caused by blood trapped in the penis and should be treated immediately to avoid permanent injury. If untreated, it may harm the man's ability to have normal erections. To treat priapism, doctors may use drugs to thin the blood or to lower blood pressure, or they may perform surgery to create an alternate escape route for the blood.

Disorders of the Testicles and Scrotum

Undescended Testicles   Testicles develop inside the body and normally move down into the scrotum before birth. Sometimes, one or both testicles fail to fully descend. The testicles can be clearly felt if they are in their proper positions in the scrotum. Testicles should move into the scrotum by the time a child is a few years old. If this does not happen, the testicle can be lowered into place surgically. It is important to understand that normal testicles may retract, or move upward, as protection against very cold temperature or against possible injury. Having testicles draw up out of the way of discomfort is in no way a symptom of undescended testes.

Hypospadias   In some males, the penis does not develop correctly. The urethra, which should open at the tip of the penis, may instead open on to its underside. This condition, known as *hypospadias,* causes the penis to take on a bow shape and to be shorter than normal. Hypospadias usually can be corrected by surgery.

Torsion of the Testicle   Normally, one testicle hangs lower and more horizontally than the other. They are suspended in the scrotum by the spermatic cord. It is possible for a testicle to experience *torsion,* or twisting, because of an injury or sometimes for no apparent reason.

When this happens, there is sudden intense pain followed by swelling and tenderness in the scrotum caused by the interruption of the blood flow in the testicle. If this occurs, the man should seek immediate medical attention. Left untreated, the entire organ may be permanently damaged. Sometimes, the testicle will untwist on its own, but it is important to consult a doctor for this condition because it may happen again. The testicle may have to be untwisted surgically and stitched into place so that it does not twist again.

Cancer of the Testicle   The most common cancer in men in their twenties and thirties is cancer of the testicle. In about half of the cases, testicular cancer does not produce pain or any other symptoms. A malignant growth might develop without being noticed until it poses a danger. Once it reaches a certain size, the tumor can grow very quickly and needs immediate medical attention. A simple self-examination may help discover a growing tumor when it is in a very early stage of development.

Self-examination of the testicles is best done after a warm bath or shower, when the scrotum is loose and relaxed. The entire surface of each testicle should be felt with the fingertips and the thumb. Any lumps, hardening, or swelling should be reported to a doctor without delay.

One testicle may become larger or heavier than the other. Any unusual change in the testicles should be examined by a doctor because untreated cancer can spread quickly to the rest of the body. But testicular cancer that is detected at an early stage can be treated with drugs, radiation, or surgery. Should an affected testicle have to be removed, the other one is very likely to remain healthy and functioning. A man with only one testicle can produce sperm and ejaculate normally.

Other Disorders of the Testicles and Scrotum   Inflammation of the epididymis is known as *epididymitis.* It can be caused by a bacterial infection, such as *chlamydia,* that moves from the urinary tract to the sperm duct. Symptoms include fever and pain in the back of the testicles. Epididymitis is treatable with antibiotics, pain killers, bed rest, ice packs, and elevation of the scrotum. Because bacteria can be passed on, a man's sex partner should also be treated.

Another infection of the testicle is *orchitis.* It can occur as a bacterial infection as a result of improperly treated epididymitis or as a viral infection associated with the childhood disease mumps. The viral infection can lead to infertility and permanent damage to the testicles.

Disorders of the Prostate Gland

Cancer of the Prostate Gland   Prostate cancer is the second most common cancer of men in the United States, accounting for 37,000 deaths per year. It occurs more commonly in elderly men and often has no early warning symptoms. Sometimes, because the prostate is attached to the urethra, there is difficulty with urination. There may be less than normal or more frequent urination, or the bladder may not empty completely. Occasionally, there may be blood in the urine.

A cancerous prostate should be removed and hormones such as estrogen given as part of the postsurgical treatment. Estrogen can decrease the size of the cancer. If detected early in its development, this cancer has a high cure rate. That is why it is important for all men over 50 to have a rectal examination every year. By feeling the prostate through the rectum, a doctor can tell whether any unusual growths or lumps are present.

Prostatitis   An inflammation of the prostate called *prostatitis* is most commonly caused by a bacterial infection. The symptoms of prostatitis include pains in the abdomen and lower back, fever, and the need to urinate frequently. The region over the prostate gland may be tender to the touch. Prostatitis is treated with antibiotics. Bed rest usually is needed, as are six to eight glasses of water every day.

4

THE FEMALE
REPRODUCTIVE SYSTEM

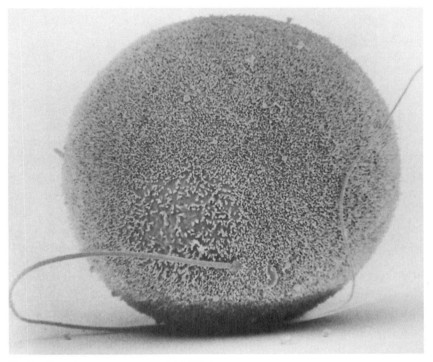

Fertilization of an ovum magnified 28,000 times

Sexual reproduction involves the participation of two parents, one male and one female. The male must manufacture sperm and then transfer it to the female. The job of the female, however, is quite a bit more complicated. Not only must she produce the egg and receive the sperm, she also must provide a protected place for the fertilized egg to develop, and she must provide the growing fetus with proper nourishment from the moment it is conceived to the time of its birth.

47

The human female reproductive system is not only more complex than the male reproductive system but it also goes through cycles that the male system does not experience. Once a man reaches puberty, his reproductive organs operate fairly consistently throughout his lifetime. As they age, the reproductive powers of all organisms, except human females, simply slow down. Other organisms breed less often and gradually produce fewer and fewer reproductive cells. Only the human female system is characterized by distinct phases. Only human females experience a cycle for the production of the egg, a cycle for the preparation of the embryo, and a final shutting down of the reproductive mechanism.

THE FEMALE EXTERNAL ORGANS

The female genitals are known as the *vulva*, meaning "covering." The vulva is the entrance both to the urinary tract and to the internal reproductive organs. Female genitals do not look the same in all women. They are as varied in appearance as the features that make one person's face different from another's. Each organ of the vulva may have its own unique size, shape, and even color. But the genitals of all women have the same general location and do the same job.

Mons Veneris The area over the pubic bone, directly beneath the stomach region, is called the *mons veneris* (from the Latin for "mound of Venus"). The mons is covered with skin, and later, starting in puberty, with pubic hair. It is a cushion of fatty tissue with many nerve endings that make the mons very sensitive to touch and stimulation.

Labia Majora Two large folds of skin form the outer lips, or *labia majora*, of the vulva. These folds cover a large layer of fat and a thin layer of muscle tissue. The outer labia, which develop pubic hair on the sides during puberty, have many sweat glands, oil glands, and nerve endings. They usually are folded together, acting as a protection for the opening to the urethra and the entrance to the internal organs.

Labia Minora Inside the outer folds are two hairless inner lips, or *labia minora*. The inner lips are curved much like the petals of a flower. Their spongy tissue has many small blood vessels and many nerve endings. These inner lips meet at the front of the genital region to form a fold of skin known as the *clitoral hood.*

Clitoris   The *clitoris is* a very sensitive organ located right under the point where the inner lips meet. The head, or *clitoral glans,* can be seen if the hood that covers it is gently pushed aside. Its *shaft is* made of spongy erectile tissue, similar to that in the penis, that fills with blood during sexual arousal. It branches in a V-shape inside the body into two longer parts known as *crura.* Because of its many nerve endings, the clitoris is very sensitive to touch, pressure, and temperature. The clitoris is involved in all female orgasms.

Vestibule   The area between the labia minora and the vagina contains the opening to the urethra and two small glands called *Bartholin's glands.* These glands are responsible for keeping the vagina moist.

THE INTERNAL REPRODUCTIVE ORGANS

Just like the external organs, the internal reproductive organs vary in size and exact positioning from woman to woman.

Hymen   The opening of the vagina is covered by a thin tissue called the *hymen.* The hymen is not the same in all females. It may form a ring around the opening to the vagina, or form separate bands that stretch across the opening. In some females, this membrane stretches completely across the vaginal opening. Whatever its size, shape, or thickness, the hymen always has many small openings.

Some females are born with only a partial hymen, and others have none at all. The first time a penis enters the vagina, an intact hymen may be torn, so that the opening becomes unobstructed. Many people mistakenly believe that an intact hymen is a sign of virginity. In fact, the hymen may be missing in the first place or may be broken at an early age by various exercises.

Vagina   The vagina is a muscular tube that leads into the other internal organs. It tilts upward into the body at a 45-degree angle, pointing toward the lower back. The walls of the vagina have a surface much

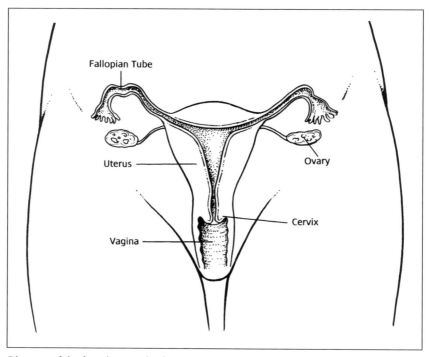

Diagram of the female reproductive system

like the inside of the mouth. The mucous membranes that line the walls help keep the vagina lubricated, preparing it for penetration by the penis. It is through this small tube that sperm enter the female.

The walls of the vagina are about 12.5 centimeters (5 inches) long. These walls have a rich supply of blood vessels, but, except for the opening and the first third, they have relatively few nerve endings. This keeps the inside of the vagina from being overly sensitive to touch or pain. The vaginal walls act as a passageway for a baby during childbirth. They can contract and expand to change the size and the shape of the vagina.

Cervix   The opening to the uterus is called the *cervix.* It is large enough to allow sperm into the uterus and menstrual blood out, but it is too small to permit tampons or other things into the uterus.

Uterus   Part of the cervix is the uterus, or womb, in which a fetus may grow to full size during pregnancy. The bottom part, or neck of the uterus, extends into the upper end of the vagina. Mucus is regularly secreted by many glands in the thin tube between the mouth of the cervix and the uterus, called the *endocervical canal.*

The uterus itself is a hollow, thick-walled organ shaped somewhat like an inverted pear. It is about 7.5 centimeters (3 inches) long and 5 centimeters (2 inches) wide, although size varies from woman to woman and may change after a woman has given birth. In two-thirds of women, it is tilted forward; in one-third, backward. It is held loosely in the pelvic region by connective tissue. The muscular part of the uterus, or *myometrium,* contains the strongest muscle fibers in the human body. They are able to stretch as a fetus grows larger, contract to push the baby outward at birth, and shrink back to their original size within a few weeks.

The inside lining of the uterus is the *endometrium.* If a woman is not pregnant, this lining is shed monthly during menstruation. For a woman to become pregnant, this lining must be prepared to receive a fertilized egg.

Fallopian Tubes   On both sides, the uterus is attached to the *fallopian tubes,* or oviducts. These tubes are about 10 centimeters (4 inches) long and form funnels at their far ends with fingerlike edges, or *fimbria.* Inside, the fallopian tubes are lined with thin folds of tissue covered by tiny hairlike structures, or *cilia.* If fertilization takes place, the sperm and egg will usually meet in these tubes, which pick up eggs released by the ovaries.

Ovaries   The ovaries are the gamete-producing organs—the gonads—of the female system. One oval ovary is located on each side of the uterus, and is approximately 3 x 2 x 1.5 centimeters (1.2 x 0.8 x 0.6 inches) in size. During *ovulation,* the two ovaries alternate in producing and releasing a ripe egg cell approximately once a month. The egg enters the fallopian tube through the fimbria. The ovaries also produce hormones important in reproduction, including estrogen and progesterone.

THE BREASTS

The breasts, or *mammary glands,* are part of both the male and female anatomy. Although not technically part of the reproductive system, they produce milk for a newborn baby, a process controlled by hormones of the reproductive system.

Women's breasts begin to enlarge during puberty. Sometime around the age of 10 or 11, buds of fatty tissue begin to form under the nipples at the tips of the breasts. For the next few years, an increasing amount of fatty tissue enlarges the breasts as well as the nipples, which have many nerve endings. The dark skin of the nipple eventually extends one or two centimeters onto the surface of the breast itself, forming a circular *areola.*

Breasts, much like the other external organs, vary from woman to woman. Whatever their outer size or shape, all breasts are the same inside. Each breast is primarily a sweat gland and contains between 15 and 20 lobes, or clusters of glandular tissue. The fatty and fibrous tissue around the lobes give the breasts their softness.

Each lobe in the breast drains into a duct that opens on the surface of the nipple. Normally, the lobes and ducts are small, and contain only some clear fluid. However, because of hormonal changes during pregnancy, they enlarge and eventually produce milk.

THE MENSTRUAL CYCLE

When her body is ready, a young girl begins a repeating cycle of activity that will prepare her body for reproduction. This is the *menstrual cycle.* During each reproductive cycle, one egg is released from an ovary into the adjoining fallopian tube. The menstrual cycle begins at puberty and continues over and over for the next 30 or 40 years. The female body prepares for this reproductive cycle long before puberty begins. A female fetus produces millions of cells that will become eggs. Although these cells are not fully developed eggs, they are all that will ever be produced. Once a female is born, she will produce no new eggs for the remainder of her life. Most of the eggs that are produced by the developing female fetus will degenerate and die rather quickly. By the time she is born, she will have only about 400,000 eggs left.

As a young girl grows up, she continues to lose more and more of the original egg supply. One egg is released every month for 30 or 40 years—a total of between 360 and 480 eggs; thus, a female is born with a huge oversupply of eggs.

The menstrual cycle repeats itself about every 28 days. It begins when the hypothalamus stimulates the pituitary gland to produce *follicle-*

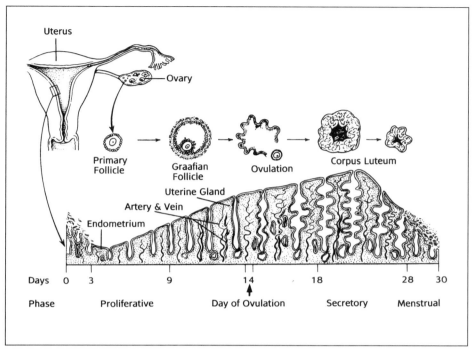

This diagram of the menstrual cycle shows the changes in thickness of the endometrium throughout the 28-day cycle and the simultaneous development and release of the ovum. The two ovaries usually ovulate in alternate months.

stimulating hormone (FSH). The FSH travels in the blood to the ovaries. There, it triggers the maturation of as many as 20 eggs. Only one of these eggs actually will become a mature ovum. During its growth, an egg divides into four cells; one of these cells is the ovum. The other three cells, called *polar bodies,* eventually degenerate. An ovum and the jellylike material that surrounds it can hardly be seen by the naked eye.

Normally, a mature ovum is produced in only one ovary at a time. However, once in a while, both ovaries produce eggs during the same cycle. If both of these eggs are fertilized, they will become fraternal twins. Identical twins develop from one fertilized egg. In the rarer event that either ovary releases several eggs at once, there is the possibility of a multiple birth, such as triplets.

The ovum is soon surrounded by a swelling bundle of cells called the *Graafian follicle,* which gets larger and larger inside the ovary, until it is almost a half inch in diameter. Now, the pituitary gland generates *luteinizing hormone* (LH), which activates the follicle to move toward the surface of the ovary. It then ruptures and passes a few inches into the fallopian tube. This is ovulation.

After the egg is released, the follicle in which it was held continues to get larger. It forms a temporary gland in the ovary called the *corpus luteum.* For 12 or 14 days following ovulation, the corpus luteum releases the important hormone progesterone. Progesterone and another hormone, estrogen, are responsible for many of the body changes that take place during the menstrual cycle.

At the onset of the cycle, when eggs begin to mature, the ovaries begin to produce estrogen. This stimulates a change in the endometrium. In the eight days that it takes for ovulation to occur, the normally thin endometrium thickens to three millimeters. For 14 days after ovulation, progesterone stimulates more changes in the uterus.

Additional layers are added to the endometrium, which increases to five millimeters (or one-fifth of an inch). Glands and blood vessels, which will help to nourish the developing baby, also enlarge. With these changes, the uterus prepares itself to receive a fertilized egg. If an egg becomes fertilized, it will travel for about a week through the fallopian tube and enter the uterus. Once there, the egg will be implanted in the thick layers of the endometrial lining.

If fertilization takes place, the female is pregnant. If there is no pregnancy within two weeks of ovulation, the corpus luteum disintegrates and disappears. With no progesterone to encourage more growth, and no egg to protect, the thick lining of the uterus is expelled from the body. This shedding of endometrial material is called menstruation. This blood loss, commonly called a "period," is mixed with patches of endometrium and mucus.

Menstrual blood leaves the body through the vagina. A number of women experience cramps in the lower abdomen when the flow begins. A menstrual period can last anywhere from two days to a week. It marks the ending of the menstrual cycle. Menstruation may be very regular in some women and very unpredictable in others.

A special medical problem that is directly related to menstruation, *premenstrual syndrome,* or PMS, refers to a varied group of problems that women may experience sometime between ovulation and the beginning of menstrual bleeding. No one ever has all the symptoms at once. In most women, PMS shows up mildly only once in a while. About 40% have PMS regularly. However, between 10% and 15% of women have very serious physical or psychological symptoms. Their pain and discomfort may be great enough to disrupt their life.

Among the most common symptoms of PMS are tension, irritability, fatigue, depression, mood swings, confusion, forgetfulness, clumsiness, and crying for no known reason. Other symptoms include bloating, swollen breasts, constipation, headaches, backaches, and pimples. The symptoms disappear as soon as women begin to menstruate. One of the doctors who pioneered the research in this field was Dr. Katharina Dalton. She studied the complaints of thousands of premenstrual women in the early 1950s. Dalton's work at University College Hospital in London underscored the connection between the symptoms women had and their menstrual cycle. The first American PMS clinic was founded by Dr. Ronald V. Norris in 1981. Today, PMS specialists all over the world have found ways to help women with PMS. Treatment methods include special diets and vitamins, stress reduction, and exercises. Some women who suffer from severe PMS may be given hormone medications.

MENOPAUSE

After the age of 40, many women do not ovulate as often as they did when they were younger. Their ovaries do not respond as easily to the chemical messages sent out by hormones. Often, their menstrual cycles become less regular. Somewhere between the ages of 48 and 52, ovulation and the menstrual flow of most women will stop forever. The ending of menstruation is known as *menopause.*

Menopause, or *climacteric* in medical terminology, is a process that may take several years to complete. When menopause begins, the menstrual cycle first becomes irregular and then stops altogether. It is difficult to determine which period is the last. Only after a year without a menstrual period can a woman be reasonably certain that she can no longer become pregnant.

During menopause, the ovaries stop producing progesterone entirely and secrete only very tiny amounts of estrogen. Most women experience some symptoms of the changes that are taking place in their body. The most common symptom is a hot flash, or sudden feeling of warmth over the upper part of the body; she may redden and become sweaty. Some women also feel slightly dizzy.

Hot flashes are not the same in all women. They may last a few seconds or a few minutes. They may occur once a week or once every hour. In most cases, the flashes stop after a year or two. In about 25 to 50% of women they last 5 or more years.

Another symptom of the menopause is vaginal dryness. This happens because fewer lubricants are secreted in the vaginal tract when menstruation ceases. In addition, the lower amount of estrogen makes the vaginal tissue less flexible than before.

Some 20% of women experience no menopausal symptoms whatsoever. The majority weather the symptoms with little more than mild discomfort. But some women find menopause a difficult experience and have to seek medical help. Doctors choose to treat some women by replacing some of the estrogen their body has stopped producing.

Estrogen replacement therapy (ERT) has caused considerable controversy in the last few years. Some doctors are concerned that it increases the risk of breast and uterine cancers. However, others are convinced that it is a safe and effective therapy. Taking progesterone in addition to estrogen reduces the risk of uterine cancer. For women who are at high risk of developing breast cancer, ERT may not be appropriate. The decision for or against ERT should be made jointly by the physician and the woman who is seeking treatment.

DISORDERS OF THE FEMALE REPRODUCTIVE SYSTEM

Problems may arise in the female reproductive system even though there is no pain or any real symptom. A regular visit to a gynecologist can assure a woman that everything is in order. A visit to a gynecologist usually includes a pelvic examination. The doctor or nurse can gently push the vaginal walls aside with a speculum. In this way, he or she has a good view of the inside of the vagina and the cervix. By touching and applying slight pressure, he or she also can determine many things about the condition of the ovaries and the fallopian tubes.

In addition to regular checkups, it is important to be able to recognize the symptoms that warn women that something may be wrong. Early detection and treatment offer the best chance for clearing up most problems in the female organs. Diseases that are transmitted primarily through sexual contact are discussed in Chapter 5.

Generalized Disorders

Toxic Shock Syndrome   A severe, sometimes fatal, illness found almost exclusively in menstruating women using tampons is *toxic shock syndrome* (TSS). It is characterized by sudden high fever, vomiting, and diarrhea, in the worst cases followed by severe shock. It may be caused by a *Staphylococcus aureus* infection. It has also been theorized that use of contraceptive sponges can increase a woman's chance of TSS.

Pelvic Inflammatory Disease   Pelvic infections involving the female's upper genital tract beyond the cervix are known by the general term *pelvic inflammatory disease* (PID). They have a range of causes and may be minor, serious, or even fatal. It is a great cause of infertility in women because it often leaves scar tissue when it heals.

Disorders of the Vagina

Vaginal Infections   It is perfectly normal for the vagina to release a colorless and odorless discharge at different times. A secretion that has an unpleasant odor or that causes itching or soreness is probably a sign of vaginal infection.

Vaginitis is an infection usually caused by the fungus *Candida* or the bacterium *Gardnerella.* Vaginitis is actually a group of infections with similar causes and symptoms. They are often called yeast infections.

Vaginitis caused by the *Candida* fungus is called *candidiasis;* that caused by *Gardnerella is* known as *bacterial vaginitis.* Both cause a thick white vaginal discharge and soreness of the outer parts of the vagina. These infections are sometimes the result of taking antibiotics or other medications that kill bacteria controlling the growth of the *normal flora,* the organisms that normally inhabit a woman's vagina. Candidiasis is usually treated with an antifungal cream. Candidiasis and bacterial vaginitis can be transferred from one sexual partner to another. Most men have no symptoms of infection; when they do, it is only a minor irritation of the penis.

Vaginitis can be caused by low estrogen levels during menopause, or it can occur for unknown reasons. Like the common cold, it is theorized that stress, poor diet, lack of sleep, or other drains on the immune system can spark vaginitis.

Prolapse   If part of the vagina or the uterus slips out of place, the condition is called a prolapse. This happens because the ligaments that hold the organs in position weaken. If the front wall of the vagina falls, or prolapses, urine may escape from the bladder if the woman coughs or sneezes. If the back wall slips down, there often is discomfort in the rectum. If the uterus follows, there may be pain and a dragging sensation. If this happens, the cervix can be felt at the opening to the vagina.

Exercises that tighten the pelvic muscles may help to relieve symptoms of a prolapse. Sometimes it is helpful to avoid strenuous activity, to stop smoking, and to lose weight. However, the only real cure for a prolapse is to operate on the tissues and ligaments that are involved.

Disorders of the Cervix

Cervical Erosion   Sometimes, cells from the inner lining spread to cover the tip of the cervix. These cells are more delicate than those that normally cover the tip, leaving the cervix open to frequent infection. This condition, known as *cervical erosion,* is not itself a disease but may cause heavy bleeding and discharge after sexual intercourse. To treat this area, it must often be cauterized.

Cervical Cancer   Cervical cancer is the second most common cancer in women (breast cancer is first). There are two forms of cervical cancer: *carcinoma in situ* (CIS) and *invasive cancer of the cervix* (ICC). In CIS, the malignant cells are on the surface of the cervix. In ICC, the cancerous cells invade the surrounding tissue.

Neither form of cervical cancer has any true symptoms, but both can be detected with a simple test. A *Pap smear* (named for Dr. George Papanicolaou, who invented it) is given during a routine gynecological examination. Cells are taken from the cervix and examined under a microscope. CIS really is not a true cancer. It takes about eight years for this precancerous condition to become a full-blown malignancy. A Pap smear can detect CIS years before it blossoms. If treated at this point, CIS has almost a 100% cure rate. The cure rate for ICC depends on how far the cancer has spread. If detected early enough, it, too, is totally curable.

Disorders of the Uterus

Fibroids   Benign muscular growths called *fibroids* are sometimes found in the wall of the uterus. Many women do not know they have a problem and find out about the fibroids during a routine examination by a physician. However, some women suffer from *menorrhagia,* or heavy menstrual bleeding. Their menstrual flow may last for 10 days or more and may show bright red bleeding with clots.

Polyps   The uterus may also be the site of growths called *polyps.* They are growths on stalks, which can be removed by a procedure called a *dilation and curettage* (D&C). This is a minor operation in which the cervix is dilated, or widened. Then an instrument is inserted into the uterus to scrape away the polyps.

Endometriosis   Occasionally, pieces of the endometrium break off and develop in another place. When *endometriosis* is present, pieces of lining may grow on the ovaries, the fallopian tubes, over the uterus, and even around the rectum or appendix. Each month, the pieces of endometrium bleed as if they were still part of the uterine lining. This causes blistering and scarring and sometimes severe pain. Endometriosis may be treated with hormones or, in severe cases, with surgical removal of the displaced pieces.

Uterine Cancer   Women, especially those over 55, may develop uterine cancer. A major symptom of this rather uncommon cancer is bleeding or abnormal discharge after menopause. Any unusual bleeding or discharge should be reported to a doctor. If cancer is diagnosed, the uterus may have to be removed surgically. Radiation therapy may also be prescribed.

The surgical procedure for the removal of the uterus is called a *hysterectomy.* During a hysterectomy, the uterus is removed through an incision low in the abdomen. Sometimes, the uterus is reached through the vagina. This is a major operation, and most women need 6 to 12 weeks to recover.

Disorders of the Ovaries and Fallopian Tubes

Cysts   The many hormonal changes in the ovaries sometimes cause *cysts* to develop. Cysts are closed sacs of nonliving tissue. They are usually filled with calcium, fluid, or blood. Small ovarian cysts may be painful at times, but they often come and go without treatment. A woman with larger cysts may feel a great deal of internal pressure. Such cysts may have to be removed surgically.

Salpingitis   Low abdominal pain and nausea, accompanied by vaginal bleeding and discharge, may indicate infections in the fallopian tubes. This disorder, known as *salpingitis,* is treated with antibiotics. Tubal infections may take a long time to clear up and may leave the patient with some discomfort even after the infection has been cured. Scarring from such infections is a cause of infertility in women.

Ovarian Cancer   Ovarian cancer is a relatively rare cancer but it can be fatal if not detected in early stages. The symptoms—lower back or abdominal pain, a bloated feeling, indigestion, weight gain, and general fatigue—could be the result of so many other problems that ovarian cancer is very difficult to diagnose.

Early detection is the key to successful treatment, but even those cases not diagnosed until later can sometimes be held in remission.

Disorders of the Breasts

Breast Cancer   Cancer of the breast is the most common cancer in women of all ages. Some women accidentally discover a painless lump in their breast. The lump may be very small or quite large and hard. It may be a harmless growth, or it may be an indication of breast cancer. Breast cancer can occur at any age and even occurs in a small number of men, but there are certain high-risk groups: women over 50, women with a mother or sister who has had breast cancer, and women who have already had breast cancer in one breast.

Doctors recommend that all women regularly examine their own breasts in front of a mirror. Self-examination is best when done at the same time every month, such as right after the period. In this way, a woman becomes familiar with the contours and bumps that are normally in her healthy breast. The things to look for during self-examination are unusual lumps, a change in the size or shape of either breast, changes in or discharge from either nipple, puckering of the skin, or unusually prominent veins.

Any change that is unusual should be brought to the attention of a doctor without delay. Many lumps that appear in the breast turn out to be benign. But some growths do turn out to be malignant. Cancer specialists all agree that the sooner a lump is diagnosed, the higher the chance for cure.

Today, most doctors also suggest that women undergo a professional breast cancer screening every year as part of their gynecological exam. This examination includes *palpation,* the feeling for lumps by trained professionals. Doctors also recommend that between ages 35 and 40 a woman have a *baseline mammogram.* Mammography uses X rays to locate tiny cancerous cells that cannot yet be felt. A baseline in this case is an X ray against which future mammograms can be compared to detect changes. Between 40 and 49, a woman should have a mammogram every year or 2. After 50, or if in a high-risk group, a woman should have a mammogram every year. All X rays, including the mammogram, expose the patient to radiation and so should not be done unnecessarily. This is why annual mammograms are not recommended for women of all ages.

Thermography is another procedure for detecting tumors early. It measures the heat given off by different parts of the body. Any changes in normal temperature patterns may be a sign of an unusual growth. This procedure does not have the radiation hazards of the mammogram, but it also cannot replace it.

Ultrasound is another detection method used. High-frequency sound waves are used to detect unusual masses in the breast. Like thermography, it is less dangerous than mammography but not as effective.

If cancer is detected, there are a number of treatment methods. Each depends on the individual woman and on the size and location of the tumor. More advanced cancers may have entered the *lymph nodes,* rounded masses of tissue containing lymph, involved in the immune system. In some breast cancers, radiation and drug therapy are effective. In other cases it may be necessary to remove the cancer surgically. There are various surgical alternatives: modified or radical *mastectomy* (removal of the breast and some or all of the lymph nodes in the armpit) or *lumpectomy* (removal of the tumor itself and any affected tissue and nodes). Whatever the treatment, the first line of defense against breast cancer is early diagnosis.

Fibrocystic Breast Disease   During the first half of the menstrual cycle, milk ducts and the supporting fibrous tissue grow. If a woman does not become pregnant, these tissues decrease again.

Sometimes, fluid is not reabsorbed and forms cysts. There are two kinds of *fibrocystic breast disease.* One is closely related to the menstrual cycle, and these cysts may disappear after a woman's period. The second type, which tends to run in families, is not in itself a serious condition, but it is often impossible to differentiate these benign lumps from cancer until they are removed and examined, and those with this disease have four times the chance of developing breast cancer as those who do not. Women should find out if there is a history of either disease in their family. And any lump should be investigated by a doctor.

5

SEXUALLY TRANSMITTED DISEASES

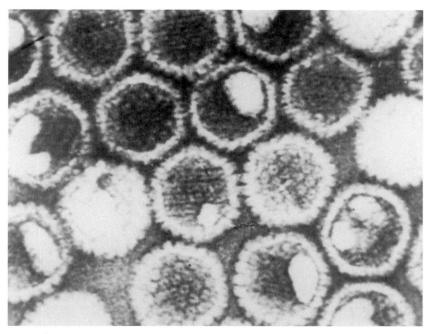

Herpesvirus

Since 1965, the world has been in the middle of an epidemic of sexually transmitted diseases (STDs). According to data compiled by the CDC, in the United States alone, 12 million new cases of STDs occur each year, at least 3 million of them among teenagers.

Billions of tax dollars each year are spent on the medical, institutional, and social costs of STDs. The human cost is even higher. As of 1998, 641,086 cases of AIDS had been diagnosed in the United States, according to the CDC, of whom 390,242 had died. STDs are also a leading cause of infertility and ectopic pregnancies in women.

CHLAMYDIA

Chlamydia is the most common STD in the United States. There are 4 million cases each year. It is caused by bacteria of the genus *Chlamydia.*

In men, the symptoms of this disorder are similar to but milder than those of *gonorrhea:* discharge and painful, frequent urination. When they seek medical attention, they are often treated for gonorrhea with penicillin only to find that it has no effect. Chlamydia is usually treated with tetracycline or doxycycline.

Chlamydia is easily transmitted to female sex partners. Many women who carry the disease have no symptoms at all. However, the infection often is found in women who complain of frequent, painful urination. This disease also can cause PID and inflammation of the cervix. It is important that the sex partner of anyone with chlamydia be examined by a doctor.

Chlamydia can by transmitted to the eye by hand-to-eye contact. If a pregnant woman has chlamydia, there is a risk that her baby can develop an eye infection or pneumonia as it passes through the birth canal. Chlamydia during pregnancy can also result in premature delivery and death.

TRICHOMONIASIS

There are 3 million cases of *trichomoniasis* each year, making it the second most common STD in the United States. This disease is often grouped together with yeast infections because of similar symptoms, but *Trichomonas,* the single-celled organism that causes it, is not part of the normal flora of the vagina or of the male urethra and is spread sexually.

Trichomonas infection causes women to have a greenish white or yellowish, foul-smelling vaginal discharge, usually accompanied by itching or burning of the vulva or vagina. Symptoms sometimes become worse right after menstruation. Many men have no symptoms of trichomoniasis, but the infection can produce pus-filled discharge and inflame the urethra and prostate. In both men and women, it can infect the bladder and cause a burning sensation when urinating. The disease is treated with the prescription drug metronidazole (trade name Flagyl). Sexual intercourse should be avoided until several weeks after the infection has healed. As this is spread sexually, medication should be taken by both partners.

GONORRHEA

Approximately 800,000 cases of gonorrhea occur annually in the United States. It is caused by a bacterium discovered in 1879 by Albert Neisser and named after him, *Neisseria gonorrhoeae.*

Most men with gonorrhea usually develop symptoms, caused by an infection in the urethra, within 2 to 10 days. There is usually a yellow discharge from the tip of the penis, along with frequent, painful urination. However, in about 10% of cases, a man with a gonorrheal infection feels no symptoms at all. He can spread the disease to his sexual partner without realizing it. If the infection is not treated, it moves up the urethra to the prostate, the seminal vesicles, and the epididymis and causes severe pain and fever.

About half the women who have gonorrhea experience no symptoms whatsoever. When there are symptoms, they often are mild and difficult to diagnose. These symptoms include a greater than usual vaginal discharge, irritation of the outer genitals, pain or burning sensation during urination, and abnormal menstrual bleeding. The lack of symptoms in so many women is a major reason for the rapid spread of this disease. Like men who experience no symptoms, women carriers easily transmit the disease through sexual intercourse. In most women with gonorrhea, the infection is in the cervix. The infection also may be found in the urethra, the rectum, and the throat. Gonorrhea in women usually spreads from the cervix to the uterus. The infection continues to the fallopian tubes and the ovaries, causing scarring that can block the tubes. This condition, a form of PID, is a major cause of infertility.

In both men and women, gonorrhea can spread to other organs through the blood vessels. It can affect the joints, the heart, and even the brain. If a mother is infected when she gives birth, the baby may develop serious eye infections. As a result, doctors put antibiotic drops into all babies' eyes at birth. If gonorrhea is diagnosed, the patient is usually given an injection of ceftriaxone or a 1-week course of oral doxycycline.

NONGONOCOCCAL URETHRITIS AND CERVICITIS

Any inflammation of the male urethra that is not caused by gonorrhea is referred to as *nongonococcal urethritis* (NGU). Approximately 50% of cases of NGU are caused by *Chlamydia trachomatis* and most of the remaining cases are caused by *Ureaplasma urealyticum.* Symptoms include painful urination and a discharge from the penis. *Nongonococcal cervicitis* refers to inflammations of the cervix not caused by gonorrhea. Most are caused by chlamydial infections, which have been discussed in a previous section.

GENITAL WARTS

These are dry, painless warts that develop around the anus or near or on the genitals. They are caused by a sexually transmitted virus, *human papillomavirus,* and appear mostly in women. There are 500,000 to 1 million cases annually in the United States.

At first, these rough, grayish white warts are very small. But they can grow to over an inch in size and become large enough to interfere with urination and bowel movement. If the warts break, they may become infected by other bacteria and become foul smelling and painful.

Genital warts may be treated by applying podophyllin ointment or liquid. They may be burned off with an electric current. This electrocautery treatment often helps prevent the warts from recurring. They may also be removed by laser or cryotherapy. Some contraceptive creams and foams also seem to be effective both in preventing and treating the warts. The condition is not considered to be a serious health problem, but women with this condition have a higher rate of cervical cancer, and if a pregnant woman with genital warts goes into labor, the delivery should be made by cesarean section.

GENITAL HERPES

Genital herpes is a highly contagious skin infection that affects the genitals of both men and women. It normally develops into a chronic, recurring, painful condition for which there is no known cure. There is no reliable statistical information, but the CDC estimates that there are 500,000 new cases every year.

Genital herpes is caused by two different forms of the *herpes simplex virus:* herpes simplex 1 and herpes simplex 2. In past years, simplex 1 was the cause of cold sores and fever blisters, whereas genital herpes was caused almost exclusively by the simplex 2 virus. Today, however, almost one-fifth of genital herpes cases can be traced to the simplex 1 virus. The disease is generally spread by direct contact with infected genitals during sexual activity. Most people with genital herpes develop clusters of small, painful, burning blisters on the genitals. In men, these appear most commonly on the penis, but they can also erupt on the urethra or rectum. In women, they usually appear on the lips of the vagina but also can affect the cervix or anus. The blisters burst after a few days, leaving open, wet reddish sores in their place. Sores on the penis will crust before they heal. Most vaginal sores, unless they become infected with another bacteria, will heal in two to three weeks.

The first time that blisters develop, it is not unusual for some people to have fever, headache, and muscle soreness for a few days. These symptoms often appear within the first four days of blistering. Other common symptoms include painful urination, vaginal or urethral discharges, and tenderness in the groin area.

The herpes simplex virus gets into nerves in the pelvic region and lives in an inactive, or dormant, state near the base of the spinal cord. In some people, there are no more attacks. But for most, especially those who carry simplex 2, the episodes recur.

The number of recurrences varies from person to person. Attacks may be repeated anywhere from every few months to every few years. In some cases, repeated attacks stop after a few years.

Generally, the recurring attacks are not as severe as the first one. Sometimes there are warning signs, such as itching or tingling in or near the genitals. The groin may become tender or painful, and urination and bowel movement may become difficult.

Attacks of genital herpes sometimes are brought on by environmental factors. They flare up after emotional stress, illness, exhaustion, or even sunburn. But, if warning signs are noticed, a person may try to get more rest, eat well, and avoid stress. Anything that may interfere with the immune system, such as drugs or alcohol, should be avoided.

Babies can be infected with herpes from the cervix or vagina during delivery. These infections can cause serious damage to the baby's brain or eyes and may even cause death. Many doctors recommend cesarean sections for pregnant women with genital herpes.

Studies have shown a higher incidence of cancer of the vulva and of the cervix in women with simplex 2. Both cancers have a high rate of cure if detected early, so it is a good idea for women with genital herpes to have regular Pap smears and pelvic examinations.

To date, there is no cure for genital herpes. Doctors may prescribe acyclovir to reduce the severity of the symptoms and to shorten the time it takes for sores to heal. Aspirin or aspirin substitutes help to ease some symptoms. Cold, wet compresses also may make people more comfortable during a flareup. It is advisable to wear loose, comfortable clothing to avoid further skin irritation. The infected area also may be washed several times a day and patted dry.

SYPHILIS

In the United States, there are over 100,000 cases of *syphilis* each year, according to the 1989 annual report of the HHS. Syphilis is caused by a spiral-shaped bacterium, *Treponema pallidum,* that was first identified in 1905.

Syphilis develops in stages. During the first two stages of the disease, it can easily be treated with one injection of penicillin. The first symptom, appearing two to four weeks after infection, is called a *chancre*

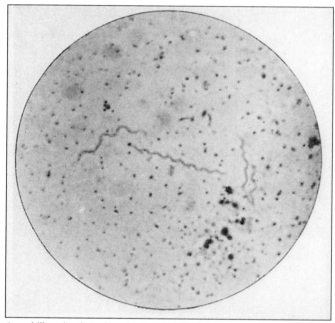

A syphilis spirochete from Vorläusiger Bericht, *written by Schaudinn and Hoffmann in 1905, the year the bacterium was discovered. This spiral-shaped microorganism causes an STD that affects over 100,000 Americans annually.*

(pronounced "shanker"). This round or oval sore often is painless and begins as a dull red spot that develops into a red-rimmed pimple. A chancre most often forms on the genitals or the anus, but it also can develop on other parts of the body.

The chancre usually heals within a few weeks, and most people believe that the infection has gone away. Unfortunately, if there has been no medical treatment, in one to six months the secondary stage of syphilis sets in. During the secondary stage, a pink rash may appear on the palms of the hands or the soles of the feet. The infected person comes down with a fever, sore throat, headaches, and pains in the joints. There is a loss of appetite, weight, and hair. Moist sores may erupt around the genitals or anus. These sores, called *condyloma lata,* are very contagious. Like chancres, they also heal and disappear.

After all of the symptoms have disappeared, syphilis can no longer be transmitted to another person. The disease goes into a latent stage. Diagnosed at this point, its treatment will involve larger doses of penicillin over a longer period of time. During the latent stage, the syphilis bacteria can burrow into and cause lesions in body tissues such as the brain, the spinal cord, blood vessels, and bones.

Many people with untreated syphilis stay in this stage for the rest of their life. Others go into late syphilis, called the tertiary stage. People in this stage of the disease may develop serious heart problems, eye disorders, and damage to their brain or spinal cord. Late syphilis can cause paralysis, blindness, insanity, and death.

Syphilis usually is transmitted by sexual contact but can also be acquired from a contaminated blood transfusion or through sharing needles used for intravenous (IV) drugs, and it can be transmitted to a fetus from an infected mother. This *congenital syphilis* can cause deformities in bones and teeth, kidney problems, and other abnormal conditions. It also can result in blindness, deafness, or death. However, if a woman with syphilis is given proper medical treatment before the 16th week of pregnancy, congenital syphilis can be prevented.

AIDS

AIDS is the newest and most frightening STD in medical history. The first cases of this devastating disease were identified in 1981. By 1985, the CDC had recorded 23,096 cases. By 1990, the total had risen to almost 200,000 cases. As of 1998, over 640,000 cases of AIDS were

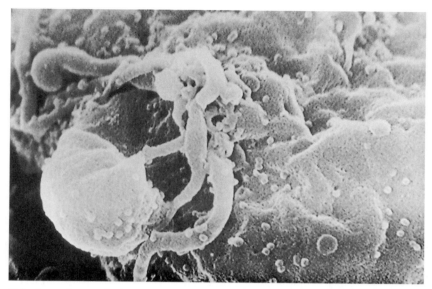

This photomicrograph shows HIV magnified 150,000 times. HIV belongs to a class of viruses called retroviruses. Today, retroviruses are being studied intently in hopes of finding a way to treat AIDS.

recorded, of whom over 390,000 had died. Worldwide, it is estimated that over 30 million people were living with HIV/AIDS.

AIDS is an infectious disease caused by the *human immuno-deficiency virus* (HIV). The virus attacks the immune system, leaving the body unprotected from a number of often fatal infections. Two of these infections are *pneumocystis carinii pneumonia* (PCP) and *Kaposi's sarcoma* (KS), a rare cancer.

Anyone who is infected with the AIDS virus develops HIV *antibodies*. Antibodies are substances in the blood that fight bacteria, viruses, and other foreign bodies. Unfortunately, HIV antibodies cannot destroy the AIDS virus. Doctors have developed tests for these antibodies, but the tests are imperfect because people may not develop antibodies for six months to several years after exposure to the virus.

Some people who are infected with AIDS become ill but do not contract KS, PCP, or any of the other diseases commonly found in AIDS patients. These people are said to have *AIDS-related complex,* or ARC. Doctors do not yet know whether or not all ARC patients eventually will develop and die of AIDS.

HIV lives in body fluids, including semen, vaginal secretions, and blood—it has not been proven that tears, saliva, or sweat can transmit the virus. It can be spread only by sexual contact or blood-to-blood contact with the body fluids of an infected person. The two most common ways of getting AIDS are by having sex with an infected person and by sharing IV needles, often used by drug addicts. AIDS is also spread when infected blood is transfused into another person and when infected pregnant women pass the disease to their babies.

Symptoms for AIDS are the same as those for many other illnesses. For some people, they are similar to those of a cold or the flu, but they hang on longer or keep coming back. Some of the most common symptoms are persistent, unexplainable fatigue; weight loss; profuse sweating at night; swollen lymph glands on the neck, under the arms, or in the groin; purple patches on the skin; watery bowel movements; white patches inside the mouth; and long-lasting fever, coughs, or headaches. Although there is no cure, new drugs are extending the lives of people with AIDS. Azidothymidine (AZT) and pentamidine are two drugs that have helped some patients with AIDS live longer. AZT was the first AIDS drug approved by the Food and Drug Administration (FDA). Pentamidine inhalers administer the drug directly into the lungs and are used in the treatment of PCP, which causes 70% of AIDS deaths.

Anyone can get AIDS. However, because of the ways in which the disease is transmitted, some people have a greater risk of getting AIDS than others. Among men diagnosed with AIDS, most acquired the infection through homosexual activity or intravenous drug use. Most women with AIDS acquired the infection through heterosexual activity or intravenous drug use. However, a person who is not in a high-risk group is not safe from AIDS. As the epidemic grows, so will the numbers and types of risk groups. As a result, it is very important that everyone takes this disease seriously and helps to stop or at least slow down its spread.

All people who are sexually active should choose their sex partners carefully; limit the number of sex partners they have; and use a latex condom, preferably one with a spermicide containing 5% nonoxynol-9, every single time they have sex. Observing these guidelines is no guarantee, however. Right now, the only way of eliminating any risk of getting this disease from a sex partner is to abstain from sex altogether. Short of that, practicing "safe" sex will, at the very least, reduce the chances of getting AIDS.

Drug users can help stop the spread of AIDS by stopping their drug use. Anyone who cannot stop using drugs must give up injecting them. If that, too, is impossible, he or she must never share a needle with anyone else. And finally, if there is no way out but to share a needle, the user must clean the needle and syringe with bleach and then rinse it thoroughly with clear water.

Understanding the symptoms and treatments of STDs is only one important step in combating their spread. It is up to each person to practice safe and responsible sex by taking steps to reduce the spread of sexually transmitted diseases: be informed, be selective, be honest, be cautious, be tested, and be treated.

6

FAMILY PLANNING

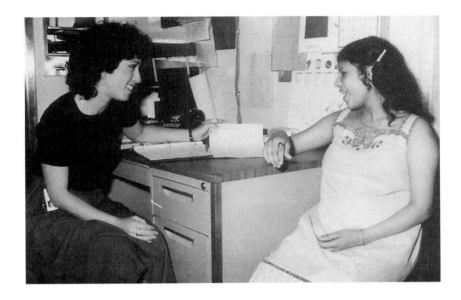

Having a baby is serious business. It is a responsibility that takes a great deal of time, energy, and money. Under the right circumstances, becoming pregnant can be a time of joy and celebration. Under the wrong circumstances, it can be a time of fear and desperation.

Luck and timing have been replaced with an assortment of *contraceptive* products and methods that can prevent an unwanted pregnancy. Yet, many pregnancies are still unplanned.

In the United States, more than a million teenagers become pregnant each year.

Some teenagers know very little about how babies are made in the first place. But far too often, when teenagers become pregnant, it is not because they did not understand but because they did nothing to prevent it. Young people may know about contraceptives but may not have access to good medical services and advice, especially if they are poor or if there are legal restrictions on giving contraceptives or information to minors. Increased knowledge and availability of contraceptives are essential if the United States wants to lower the number of pregnancies among unmarried teenagers.

CONTRACEPTION

Once a woman has decided to use contraception, she has another choice to make: what form to use. This decision should be made in conjunction with a doctor. Some methods are safer than others for different women, some methods are more effective than others, and some methods are more expensive than others. A woman may also want to consult her partner in this decision because some methods need the cooperation of both people to be effective. In the end, however, the woman herself will suffer the side effects of the method or the resulting pregnancy if it fails, so she ought to carefully consider her own needs.

Oral Contraceptives

Birth Control Pills   When it was introduced in the mid-1950s, the pill revolutionized birth control all over the world. For the first time, pregnancy could be prevented by simply taking a pill. In the United States today, more than 9 million choose this method of birth control.

There are three basic types of oral contraceptives: the *combination pill,* the *multiphasic pill,* and the *minipill.* All three work on the same basic principle but vary somewhat in their effectiveness, their side effects, and their ingredients. In general, birth control pills contain some combination of estrogen and progesterone, or synthetic versions of these hormones, which control a woman's menstrual cycle and her body's preparations for pregnancy. Essentially, the pill works by preventing ovulation and causing the mucus in the cervix to thicken, hindering sperm from entering the uterus. Some pills also change the lining of the uterus, making implantation more difficult.

The type of pill introduced in the 1950s was very high in estrogen, and many women developed side effects. All of today's pills have considerably

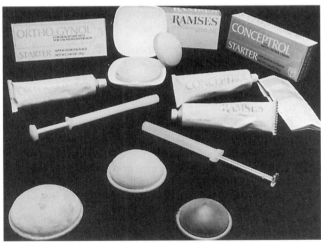

Top: *There are a variety of oral contraceptives available today.* Bottom: *Diaphragms are made in varying sizes. A woman's doctor must decide which size is right.*

lower doses of hormones and so are safer. Still, each may spark certain side effects, ranging from the minor irritation of tender breasts to serious blood clots. The chance of side effects increases if the woman is over 35 or if she smokes.

The combination pill contains two hormones, synthetic estrogen and progestin, a progesterone-like substance. There are different brands of the combination pill, containing different levels of hormones. A doctor can advise the woman on which brand might best suit her.

The multiphasic pill is really several pills, each taken during a different segment of a woman's cycle and each containing different levels of the hormones. These pills contain a lower total dose of hormones than the combination pill, so the side effects are often milder. The combination pill and the multiphasic pill are both 99% effective in preventing pregnancy.

The minipill contains a small amount of progestin and no estrogen. Women using the minipill probably ovulate occasionally, but the pill makes the mucus in the cervix so thick that sperm cannot pass through it. The minipill is 97% to 98% effective.

The "morning-after pill" refers to several types of medication sometimes prescribed after a woman has had unprotected intercourse, or if she suspects a failure with the contraceptive she was using, or in an emergency situation such as rape. To be effective, this pill must be taken within a certain amount of time after intercourse. Most of these drugs affect the uterine lining in a way that prevents implantation. It must be prescribed by a doctor and are usually used only in an emergency. The large doses of hormones in these pills may have undesirable side effects.

Some pills are taken every day, some only 21 days a month, but either way the directions must be followed exactly for the pill to work. Missing even one day when a pill should be taken can result in pregnancy.

Spermicides and Barrier Contraceptives

Barrier contraceptives, those that physically prevent the union of the sperm and egg, are most effective when used in conjunction with a *spermicide,* a chemical that kills or weakens sperm. Some spermicides may also be used alone but they are much less effective. These methods of contraception have become increasingly popular because they help prevent the spread of some STDs. Latex condoms used with spermicides containing at least 5% nonoxynol-9 may help prevent the spread of AIDS as well as STDs such as chlamydia and syphilis.

Spermicides   Foams, jellies, creams, film, or suppositories that are inserted into the vagina and kill sperm can be purchased at most pharmacies without prescriptions. Creams and jellies usually come in tubes with applicators, foams come in aerosol cans, and suppositories are foaming tablets. Vaginal contraceptive film (VCF) is the most recently developed form of spermicide. VCF is a thin, square piece of film laced with a spermicide. Like a suppository, it dissolves when inserted into the vagina. In addition to killing sperm, these substances act as a barrier between sperm and the uterus. All spermicides must be reinserted with each act of intercourse.

Most spermicides have a theoretical effectiveness of 95% to 97% but an actual effectiveness of 85% or below. Theoretical effectiveness is the rate at which a method is effective if it is used correctly and used at every instance of sexual intercourse; actual effectiveness is the rate at which a method is effective in practice, including instances when it is not used or used incorrectly. The effectiveness rate of suppositories is even lower. Most spermicides must not be put in place more than 30 minutes before intercourse and must not be douched away afterward. Suppositories and VCF, however, must be inserted long enough before intercourse to properly dissolve. Adverse side effects may include allergic reactions and burning and itching of the penis and vagina.

Condoms   A *condom is* a thin, elastic sheath that fits snugly over an erect penis, catching sperm during intercourse. The theoretical effectiveness for condoms alone is 90% to 97%, and 99% when used with a spermicide, but the actual effectiveness for both is 80% to 85%. Although condoms are not the most effective method of birth control, they are highly recommended for use against STDs, including AIDS, and can be used in conjunction with other contraceptive methods.

Condoms are available with or without a lubricant. Lubricants, especially spermicidal lubricants, are recommended because they lessen the chance of breakage during intercourse. Some condoms have a plain, rounded end; others have a nipplelike reservoir at the tip to collect semen. Reservoir-tip condoms may better resist breakage. Condoms are made of latex rubber or natural lambskin. The AIDS virus can pass through tiny pores in lambskin, so a latex condom must always be used.

This 1987 photo shows a Stanford University senior handing out "safe sex kits" containing condoms. Increased condom use has been advocated by both private groups and the government to slow the spread of STDs, especially AIDS.

The CDC recommends the use of condoms with vaginal spermicides that contain nonoxynol-9, specifically the use of a nonoxynol-9-lubricated latex condom or a nonlubricated latex condom with a separate nonoxynol-9 vaginal contraceptive.

These combinations are probably the best protection against contracting AIDS during intercourse.

Condoms can break or tear, often because they have not been handled properly. Condoms should not be stored in hot places or in sunlight because the rubber will deteriorate. Petroleum jelly (Vaseline), massage oil, or oil-based lubricants should never be used with a condom. They can weaken the latex in a few minutes. A water-based lubricant meant for use with condoms should be used. A condom that is more than a year old or that is in a torn or open packet should not be used, and a condom should never be reused.

Diaphragm   A *diaphragm* is a round, shallow rubber dome stretched over a flexible ring. It is used with spermicidal jelly or cream and is inserted into the vagina so that it covers the cervix. The rubber cup forms a mechanical barrier between the uterus and the sperm and holds the spermicide, which acts as a chemical barrier.

When properly used with a spermicide, the diaphragm's effectiveness is 98%. When misused or used sporadically, effectiveness drops to 80%. A woman must insert it no later than two hours before intercourse and keep it in place for at least six hours afterward. In order to be properly protected, a woman must be fitted for a diaphragm by a doctor. Spermicide must be reinserted with each act of intercourse or if a long period of time passes after insertion.

A diaphragm is an effective, safe contraceptive, but there are things that may go wrong. It can slip out of place during intercourse, or a tiny hole can allow sperm to pass through. Inspect it carefully before insertion and check its position before intercourse.

Cervical Cap   The *cervical cap* is similar to a diaphragm but smaller and thicker, fitting snugly over the cervix. It can be left in place for up to three days with no additional application of spermicide. It is comparable in effectiveness to the diaphragm. Drawbacks include a limited number of available sizes, the possibility of it becoming dislodged during intercourse, or vaginal discharge if it is left in place too long.

Contraceptive Sponges   *Contraceptive sponges* are soft, disposable, polyurethane sponges about two inches in diameter, saturated with the spermicide nonoxynol-9. The sponge is moistened and inserted into the vagina like a tampon. It can be put in place up to four hours before intercourse and must be left in place for six hours afterward. The sponge acts as a physical barrier, absorbs semen, and contains a spermicide. Theoretical effectiveness is believed to be 90% but the actual rate in a preliminary study was only 83%. Some sponges are suspected of increasing the risk of TSS.

Intrauterine Device

The *intrauterine device* (IUD) is a small device inserted by a physician into the uterus through the cervix. It prevents pregnancy by interfering with the implantation of the fertilized egg in the wall of the uterus. Effectiveness is 94% to 99%. Once widely used, the IUD has become less common and more controversial. IUDs have been linked to the increased incidence of PID because they have a thin "tail" that hangs through the cervix and may provide a pathway for bacteria and viruses to enter the uterus. IUDs may also cause sterility, *ectopic* (outside the uterus) pregnancy, or perforation of the cervix or uterus. Because of these problems and related lawsuits, only one brand, the Progestasert, remains on the market. The Progestasert is a small, T-shaped, plastic device containing progesterone, which is slowly released over the course of a year. After a year, the device must be replaced.

Natural Family Planning

Natural family planning requires abstinence from intercourse during the fertile time of the menstrual cycle, that is, during the days preceding and just following ovulation. It requires very careful timing to avoid the possible meeting of an egg and sperm in the woman's body. It also requires both partners to be willing to abstain totally from sex for a part of each month.

There are four ways to determine a woman's fertile period: the calendar method, body temperature method, examination of cervical mucus, and the symptothermal method. The calendar method involves careful record keeping and calculation. It is not as accurate in young women, who do not yet have completely regular cycles. The temperature method involves the daily use of a special thermometer and accurate record keeping. To use the cervical mucus method, a woman must observe her vaginal secretions daily. The symptothermal method involves observation of changes in the cervix as well as the temperature and mucus.

Effectiveness varies greatly depending on correct use. The calendar method is 53% to 86% effective, the temperature method 80% to 99%, the mucus method 75% to 90%, and the symptothermal method 78% to 99%. Using two methods together improves effectiveness.

Sterilization

Short of having no sexual relationships at all, there is only one way to guarantee full protection against pregnancy, and that is *sterilization,* the use of surgery to alter the reproductive system.

A person must be certain of his or her decision to undergo sterilization because it must be considered irreversible. A woman can be sterilized through a *tubal ligation,* or *occlusion,* (tying, blocking, or cutting the fallopian tubes) or a hysterectomy. A man can be sterilized through a *vasectomy* (cutting and tying the vas deferens, which carries sperm).

ABORTION

Sometimes, no matter how carefully contraceptives may have been used, a woman becomes pregnant without planning to. At this point, she has another decision to make. Should she give birth to and raise the child, give birth and then put the child up for adoption, or should she have an abortion? This may be one of the hardest decisions a woman will ever have to make, and, ideally, she should not have to make it alone. A woman and her partner should make a joint decision, taking into consideration their desire for a child; the stability of their relationship; their financial situation; their religious and cultural beliefs; and the availability of people who will assist with child care. In the end, this decision may affect the woman more than the man. It is in her body that a baby will grow for nine months. If her partner is not around to help make a decision, a woman may want to consult her parents, friends, health care counselors, or members of the clergy.

Women may also consider abortion if they have become pregnant through rape or incest. Or they may have planned and desired the pregnancy but then learned through genetic testing that the fetus is deformed or carries a serious genetic disease. In any case, if the decision is to have an abortion, the sooner the better.

During the first *trimester,* the first three months of pregnancy, abortion is a relatively simple medical procedure. The earlier it is done the safer and less expensive it is. In the second trimester, or fourth to sixth month, the chance of complications and the expenses increase, and the number of facilities willing to do the procedure decrease. Abortion is legal in the United States during the first and second trimesters, and in certain circumstances during the third trimester. More restrictions are imposed in various states. Some states may have restrictions such as parental notification or the requirement that second trimester abortions be performed in a hospital, making them much more expensive. The appendix in the back of this book lists agencies that can provide information on abortion, adoption, and prenatal care.

INFERTILITY

Some 10% to 15% of couples who want children run into the problem of infertility. Infertility may be caused by a problem with either partner. In women, two major causes of infertility involve a blockage in the fallopian tubes and the failure to ovulate. The most common cause

Some women who have trouble ovulating use fertility drugs to become pregnant. One side effect of these drugs is the increased chance of multiple births—twins, triplets, and still larger multiple births have been reported.

of male infertility is a low sperm count. Abnormal sperm, impaired sperm *motility* (swimming ability), and an inadequate amount of seminal fluid can also cause infertility. A man also may be infertile if his sperm has a problem penetrating an egg.

There are several medications that are given to women who do not ovulate. Climophene and human menopausal gonadotropins (HMG) have helped many such women to become pregnant. Other fertility drugs stimulate production of estrogen and progesterone or stimulate the pituitary gland to produce hormones that do so. However, taking these drugs sometimes results in multiple births. Some women with blocked tubes can be treated by microsurgery.

The treatment of male infertility is not very developed. Doctors can clear up infections or hormone disorders that may affect a man's sperm count. Limiting the number of times a man ejaculates to once in any

48-hour period has been helpful to some men. But most cases of male infertility do not respond well to specific treatments. When a man cannot produce enough sperm to impregnate his healthy partner, some doctors recommend other methods.

Alternatives

Artificial Insemination   The oldest alternative method, *artificial insemination,* involves placing sperm in the cervix by a method other than sexual intercourse. The sperm may come from the woman's partner, a friend, or an anonymous donor. Sperm banks store sperm for such purposes. The sperm may be fresh or frozen, but fresh sperm seem to be more effective because they are more motile. Artificial insemination is used if the woman's partner has a low sperm count, if his sperm carry genetic defects, if for physical or psychological reasons he is unable to ejaculate during intercourse, if he is totally infertile, or if the woman wants a child without a partner.

In Vitro Fertilization   *In vitro fertilization* (IVF) means combining an egg and a sperm in a laboratory dish and then implanting the fertilized egg in the woman's body for a normal pregnancy and birth.

Gamete Intra-Fallopian Transfer   *Gamete intra-fallopian transfer* (GIFT) involves surgically placing the egg and sperm directly into the woman's fallopian tubes for a natural conception and birth. The operation is more difficult but less time consuming and expensive than in vitro fertilization.

Embryo Transfer   In *embryo transfer,* the sperm of an infertile woman's partner is used to fertilize another woman's egg in the laboratory. This fertilized egg is then placed in the uterus of the man's partner, and she carries it to term and gives birth to the baby.

Surrogacy   *Surrogate mothers* are women who agree, sometimes for a fee, to be artificially inseminated with the sperm of an infertile woman's partner, carry the baby to term, and then legally give the baby to the man and his partner to raise. The legal rights of the various parties involved in such an arrangement can be very complicated; some states restrict or bar surrogacy, especially paid surrogacy; some states allow it.

Host Uterus   The *host uterus* method involves combining sperm and an egg from a couple, from two donors, or from one donor and one member of the couple and then implanting the fertilized egg in another woman. This woman then carries and delivers the baby and allows the couple to legally adopt it. The legal issues associated with this method have not been fully resolved.

7

PREGNANCY AND CHILDBIRTH

Human babies are created only by the joining of an egg from the female and a sperm from the male—*fertilization*. This union marks the moment of conception and the beginning of pregnancy. During pregnancy, the fertilized egg undergoes many changes, ultimately developing into a complete new baby that is ready to be born.

FERTILIZATION

The genitals of males and females are shaped by nature to help sperm cells reach a waiting egg. When a male is sexually aroused, his penis becomes erect; it becomes thicker, wider, and firmer so that it may be inserted into the vagina. When a female is sexually aroused, her vagina becomes lubricated. This helps the penis to slide inside the vaginal canal more smoothly. During sexual intercourse, the penis moves back and forth inside the vagina and eventually spurts out its sperm-filled semen.

During intercourse, men and women often experience a pleasurable feeling called an orgasm. An orgasm takes place when muscles in the pelvic area and other regions of the body release and contract in a special rhythm. Most men experience orgasm when they ejaculate. But ejaculation and orgasm are two separate processes. It is important to understand that semen can be released even if no orgasm takes place. Ejaculation, not orgasm, sends sperm cells on their way. Females may experience orgasm in a variety of ways but all are thought to involve the clitoris.

During intercourse, semen is usually deposited fairly deep in the vaginal tract. It is spurted toward the cervix of the female. Even if there is no *penetration* (entrance of the penis into the vagina), but sperm are ejaculated near the vagina, they may still enter. This means that a female can become pregnant even without intercourse.

During ovulation, an ovum is released into one of the fallopian tubes. After it has left the ovary, the mature egg can be fertilized only for a period of 36 to 48 hours. After this time, it will degenerate. Sperm can stay alive in the female's body for as many as five days. After ejaculation, about 200 million sperm are in the vagina. Only a few thousand of them ever make it to the fallopian tube, and only a few hundred sperm ever get near the egg. Some of the sperm spill out of the vagina, while others clump together and stop moving forward. Still other sperm take a wrong turn and end up in the tube that has produced no egg this time. If, by chance, eggs are released by both ovaries, the two eggs may be fertilized and grow into fraternal, or nonidentical, twins.

Only one of the sperm that survive the journey to the fallopian tubes will be able to enter and fertilize the egg. That sperm releases a chemical that dissolves part of the coating that surrounds the egg and is then helped into the egg by *microvilli,* little hairlike structures. Once the sperm has entered the egg, no other sperm can penetrate its coat.

Fertilization produces a single cell called a zygote. After about 32 hours, the zygote splits into 2 cells. Then these two cells split into four, then eight, and on and on. Each splitting results in smaller and smaller cells, until the whole cluster looks somewhat like a mulberry. After three or four days, the cluster, known as a *morula,* moves down the fallopian tube and enters the uterus. By now, it has a hollow inside that is filled with fluid, and it is called a *blastula.*

Five to nine days after conception, the blastula begins a process called implantation, attaching itself to the uterine lining. Here it will get the food and oxygen it needs during these early days.

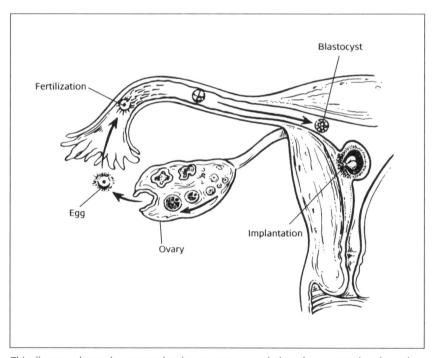

This diagram shows the ovary releasing an egg, or ovulating; the egg moving through the fimbria into the fallopian tube; being fertilized; turning into a blastocyst; and finally implanting in the endometrium, where it will develop into an embryo.

PREGNANCY

Any female who suspects she may be pregnant should consult a doctor. She might choose to visit an obstetrician, a doctor who specializes in caring for pregnant women and delivering babies, or a family practitioner also trained to assist most births. The *prenatal care* given to an expectant mother and the developing baby is very important. Having regular examinations to see that everything is going well helps ensure the delivery of a healthy baby to a healthy mother.

The most important sign that a female is pregnant is the cessation of menstruation—a missed period. A period can be delayed for a number of reasons other than pregnancy, but it is reasonable to assume that a female who has previously been regular might be pregnant if her period does not come. About half of all females have some nausea or vomiting in the early months of pregnancy. This *morning sickness* is most often felt early in the day. It usually disappears after the third month of pregnancy. Early in its formation, the embryo exerts pressure on the growing uterus. This causes pregnant females to urinate more frequently. Secretions from the vagina change throughout a pregnancy. Soon after a period is missed, a pregnant female will probably notice thick, white, sticky discharges.

None of these signs is a sure indication of pregnancy. To find out for certain, a pregnancy test can be given by a doctor, at a medical laboratory, or at a clinic. Self-testing pregnancy kits that can be used at home are available at most pharmacies. These tests identify a specific chemical in the urine, human chorionic gonadotropin (HCG), a hormone produced only in the bodies of pregnant women. The tests are 95% to 98% accurate if they are given no earlier than 2 weeks after a missed period.

Pregnancy also can be confirmed by a pelvic examination about six weeks into a pregnancy. During a pelvic examination, the doctor can observe a softening of the cervix and of the uterus just above the cervix, a bluish coloring on the vagina and cervix, and an increase in the size of the uterus.

PRENATAL DEVELOPMENT

The average pregnancy lasts 266 days. The changes that take place during this time usually are described in terms of trimesters. The em-

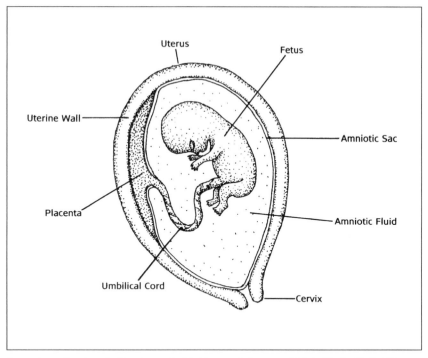

An embryo develops in the uterus, inside the amniotic sac, which is filled with fluid to cushion the embryo. Blood from the mother travels to the embryo through the placenta, providing oxygen and nutrients, and returns to the mother carrying carbon dioxide and other waste products.

bryo goes through a set of specific developmental changes during each trimester.

The First Trimester

During the first eight weeks after fertilization, the unborn baby is generally called an embryo, although, at certain specific stages of development, other terms, such as *zygote* or *blastula,* are also correct. After eight weeks, it is known as a fetus. At the outset of its first trimester of life, the blastula is less than 1 millimeter (.04 inch) in diameter. In its first weeks, it develops a placenta and *fetal membranes.* The embryo receives oxygen and nutrients from its mother through the placenta. It also passes its waste products out through this special organ.

The placenta is a smooth, flat barrier between the mother and the embryo. It produces chemicals that keep the mother's body prepared to hold the developing embryo. The placenta filters out some materials from the mother before they pass through to the baby. The placenta changes its size and thickness throughout the pregnancy to best meet the needs of the embryo.

The fetal membranes are thin sacs of tissue that enclose the embryo in a special liquid. These membranes include the *amnion,* the *chorion,* and the *allantois.* The placenta is made partly from the chorion and the allantois and partly from the uterus. The liquid in the amnion, or amniotic fluid, keeps the embryo warm and protects it against bumps and jolts. The embryo floats in this fluid throughout pregnancy.

By the end of its first month, the embryo is a quarter of an inch long and 10,000 times heavier than it was at the moment of conception. It has a crude, tubelike heart, a simple digestive system, and the beginnings of a brain and spinal cord. By the fifth week, it has the outline of eyes on its rather large head. Little buds can be seen where arms and legs will develop.

In the next two weeks, eyes, ears, and bones begin to form. At the end of seven weeks, true bone cells begin to form. Before this, the embryo skeleton is made of *cartilage,* a softer structural tissue. At 8 weeks, the embryo has grown to 3 centimeters (1.2 inches). It has hands and feet and is forming the major blood vessels. A male embryo starts to form some genital tissues. At 9 weeks, it becomes known as a fetus. By the beginning of its 12th week, it has increased in weight another 74 times.

In the final weeks of the first trimester, the fetus develops finger- and toenails, hair follicles, and eyelids. Its arms and legs grow to lengths that are in proportion to its body. The fetus develops the outer organs that show it to be either male or female. It has a functioning heart and a stomach, kidneys, and a liver. It now has all the body systems.

The Second Trimester

The fourth month marks the beginning of the second trimester. Now the fast growth rate of the earlier months slows down, but the mother's body bulges to accommodate the growing fetus. In its protected sac, the fetus continues to change. Parts of the brain differentiate. It learns to make sucking motions and moves actively in the amniotic fluid. Between the 16th and the 18th week the mother often can feel the fetus moving, or quickening. The fetus will begin to twist and kick more and more as the weeks go on.

By the fifth month, the fetal heartbeat can be heard quite clearly. The fetus is able to respond to sound and spends some of the day sleeping and some of the day staying awake. By the sixth month, the fetus develops hair on its head and forms lips and fingerprints. It can open its eyes. It has grown to 30 centimeters (12 inches) and weighs 600 to 700 grams (1.3 to 1.5 pounds).

The Third Trimester

During its third trimester, the fetus becomes more and more prepared to face the world on its own. During the seventh month, the fetus's brain and nervous system continue to develop. Most of its downy hair disappears, and fatty tissue grows under its skin. At 28 weeks, all the vital organs have been formed. Some babies are born prematurely, before their 266 days of development are completed. Only about 10% of babies survive if they are born after just 7 months of pregnancy. But, after 8 months, the chance of survival increases to about 70%.

In the eighth month, the skin of the fetus becomes smooth and pinkish. By this time, it has turned head down in the uterus, and becomes less active than before. This is because the fetus has grown to an average length of 50 centimeters (20 inches) and has less room in which to move. It receives antibodies from its mother that will protect the newborn baby from many types of infection. A few weeks before labor is to begin, the head of the fetus lowers into the pelvis.

PRENATAL CONCERNS

Every prospective parent hopes for a healthy baby. Many things can be done to ensure this. A pregnant woman must be careful about everything that she puts into her body and everything to which she exposes herself. However, there are conditions that may affect a fetus regardless of how careful a pregnant woman might be. Genetic disease and disorders may be inherited from parents or grandparents or they may stem from problems that occur during the formation of the egg or sperm cell. It is important to know what can cause a problem in a fetus and to avoid it if possible. There are tests that can detect many of these conditions. If a very serious or even fatal defect is found, the pregnant woman may consider an abortion. Even if she does not, the knowledge that her baby will be born with a problem can help her prepare herself emotionally and can help doctors prepare medically.

Inherited Disorders

Inherited disorders can come about in several ways. They can be caused by inheriting two recessive genes for a disorder or by inheriting one dominant gene. They can be sex linked, meaning that the gene for that defect is carried on the X chromosomes. Disorders can stem from defective chromosomes, or chromosomes that have mutated.

Recessive Gene Disorders   Chromosomes come in pairs. Each gene on one chromosome has an analogous gene on the other chromosome in the pair. If a person inherits one dominant and one recessive gene, the dominant trait will be expressed. This person will be a *carrier* of the recessive gene; if this is a disease gene, the person will not have the disease but can pass it on. If the person has two recessive genes, the recessive trait will be expressed. Recessive gene disorders include the following:

- *Sickle-cell anemia* occurs in about 1 out of 50 babies of African-American heritage. Its name comes from the crescent, or sickle, shape, of damaged red blood cells. These damaged cells cannot carry enough oxygen. The disease often is severe enough to cause death before 30. This disease has no known cure, but its symptoms— pain in various parts of the body—can be treated. There are tests that can tell whether a person is a carrier of sickle-cell anemia. Carriers, who have one gene for sickle-cell anemia, may exhibit mild symptoms of the disease.

- *Thalassemia* is another inherited blood disorder. It is found most often in people from Mediterranean countries: Italy, Greece, Cyprus, Syria, and Turkey. A person with thalassemia does not produce enough *hemoglobin,* the molecule in red blood cells that carries oxygen, and has very pale red blood cells. Like sickle-cell anemia, this disease is severe and may cause death in early childhood if it is inherited from both parents. It is very mild or completely without symptoms in a person who inherits thalassemia from one parent. The only way to treat this disorder is to give the patient periodic blood transfusions.

- *Tay-Sachs disease* is found among people of Jewish ancestry. It is a disorder of an *enzyme* (a chemical that causes a reaction to begin or quicken) and can be passed from a single defective gene. Tay-Sachs starts when a baby is six months old, and it affects the nervous system. It causes physical and mental retardation and blindness between the ages of 18 months and 3 years. As with sickle-cell anemia, chromosome tests can help prospective parents find out if they are carriers of Tay-Sachs disease.

- *Phenylketonuria* (PKU) is a rare inherited biochemical disease in which a vital liver enzyme is missing. The baby of two PKU carriers cannot tolerate milk. If untreated, poisons produced by milk products will cause severe brain damage and early death. Most states require a simple blood test that can detect PKU a few days after birth. Special diets and synthetic foods can help PKU children to develop normally.

Dominant Gene Disorders   Some diseases occur if only one disease gene is inherited—a dominant gene. This is true in the case of *Huntington's chorea,* a serious degenerative disease of the nervous system that is eventually fatal. Because a child need only inherit 1 gene, there is a 50% chance that a child of someone who carries the gene will receive it. The disease does not appear until middle age, by which time the patient may already have had children. Until recently, the children of a Huntington's patient had to agonize about who among them had inherited the condition. Today, a test is available that shows whether or not a person has the gene for this disease.

Sex-linked Disorders   Disorders caused by genes carried on the X chromosome appear in males more often than in females. This is because a female inherits one X from her father and one from her mother; a male inherits only one X, from his mother, and one Y, from his father. If the defect is recessive, it may not be expressed in the female child, who may inherit one X with the gene and one without it. If the male inherits an X with the disorder, it will be expressed because there is no analogous gene on the Y chromosome.

Examples of sex-linked disorders include certain types of *color blindness* and *hemophilia.* People who are color blind cannot distinguish certain colors and may see those colors as shades of gray. Hemophilia is a relatively rare sex-linked disease in which the blood does not clot properly. Most hemophiliacs have uncontrolled bleeding, even from a minor cut. People with hemophilia lack one of several *factors* in the blood that enable it to clot, factor VIII or factor IX. These essential clotting factors can be separated from the blood of healthy donors and transfused into the body of a hemophiliac. Factor VIII can also be manufactured synthetically.

Chromosome Mutations   Chromosomes can break; pieces broken off can then be lost, or become reattached in a different spot or in a different order on the chromosome they came from, or even become attached to an entirely different chromosome. When chromosomes divide during meiosis and mitosis, the new chromosomes can pair up incorrectly, even with more than two chromosomes in the "pair."

This is the cause of *Down's syndrome.* The child ends up with 3 rather than 2 chromosomes in pair 21. This disorder affects about 1 in 600 births. This chromosome error may happen for no apparent reason. However, its incidence rises with the age of the mother. A child with Down's syndrome has a set of slightly abnormal physical characteristics. Children with Down's syndrome are mentally handicapped to varying degrees and may have heart, kidney, or digestive disorders. But these children are also loving, responsive, and sweet tempered.

Environmental Factors in Pregnancy

It is important for a woman who is pregnant to know which things in her environment can be dangerous. With the proper information and care, many potential dangers to a fetus can be avoided.

Radiation and X-ray exposure can be hazardous even before a pregnancy occurs. Radiation from X rays can cause damage to chromosomes that may not show up for several generations. Because damage to genes can be inherited, the ovaries and testes should be x-rayed only when absolutely necessary.

Medications, even those prescribed by a physician, can affect the fetus. Almost every drug taken by a pregnant woman gets into the circulatory system of the fetus. Some drugs act on a particular organ of the growing fetus but are safe to use after that organ is formed. For this reason, drug use during the first half of pregnancy holds the highest risk for the baby.

Aspirin can cause bleeding in the fetus, and, if taken with caffeine and some other over-the-counter drugs, it can lead to low birth weight, anemia, and low survival rates after birth. Tranquilizers may cause physical abnormalities and heart defects in the fetus. During the 1960s, a tranquilizer called Thalidomide was widely prescribed in Europe and parts of the United States. The tragic result was severe malformations in the arms and legs of thousands of babies.

Drugs that cause malformations in the unborn child are called *teratogens*. Hormones often are teratogenic. For many years, a form of estrogen called diethylstilbestrol (DES) was taken to prevent miscarriages. Daughters of mothers who took this drug were found to have a high rate of vaginal cancer.

Antibiotics that are used to treat infections may also have adverse effects. Streptomycin may cause deafness in the fetus. Tetracycline, another commonly prescribed antibiotic, can cause the child's teeth to be permanently stained. Chloramphenicol can cause respiratory problems and circulatory collapse in newborn babies. The effects of medication often depend on how much of a drug is taken and for how long. To avoid risk, a pregnant woman should consult her doctor before taking any medication at all.

Addictive drugs such as heroin, barbiturates, amphetamines, and cocaine expose the fetus to a large number of problems. Babies of addicted mothers often are premature and have a low birth weight. In addition, the addiction is passed on to the baby. An addicted baby spends its first days of life undergoing the terrible pains of drug withdrawal.

Cigarette smoking during pregnancy has been found to have many negative effects on the fetus. Mothers who smoke during pregnancy have shortened pregnancies, higher rates of miscarriage, more complications of pregnancy and labor, higher rates of fetal death near the time of birth, and babies with lower birth weights. The effects of cigarette smoking are recognized by the surgeon general of the U.S. Public Health Service. In 1988, Dr. C. Everett Koop ordered that all cigarette packages include a warning to pregnant women.

In 1977, the FDA described a large number of severe physical and mental defects that occurred in babies of alcoholic mothers. *Fetal alcohol syndrome* (FAS) includes damage to the brain and nervous system, growth deficiencies, abnormalities of the face, bones, genitals, and heart, and mental retardation, hyperactivity, or learning deficits. Lower birth weights and more miscarriages occur among pregnant women who regularly consume alcohol during their pregnancies. Alcohol also enters breast milk. This alcohol not only is transmitted to the nursing infant but also reduces the amount of milk that the mother produces.

Infections that affect the mother may be dangerous to the developing baby. Especially dangerous are German measles (rubella) during the first or second trimester and toxoplasmosis, which is caused by a parasite found in raw meat.

MONITORING THE FETUS

Doctors can now detect the presence of certain types of defects early in pregnancy. Professional counselors can help couples who fear that they may pass genetic defects to their children. During genetic counseling, careful medical histories of both parents are taken. The couple is given information about tests that may help to determine whether they are carriers of hereditary diseases such as Tay-Sachs or sickle-cell anemia.

Amniocentesis is one of the procedures often recommended in counseling. During amniocentesis, which can be performed after 16 weeks of pregnancy, amniotic fluid is removed and tested. In the fluid there are fetal cells that are analyzed. In three to four weeks, the test results identify conditions such as Down's syndrome and muscular dystrophy, as well as the sex of the fetus and if the fetus has *Rh disease.* If the mother's blood is Rh negative and the baby is Rh positive, antibodies from the mother cross the placenta and begin to destroy the baby's red blood cells. This usually will not seriously affect a first baby. It is not until after that birth that the mother will produce antibodies. There is now a vaccine to prevent antibody formation and thus prevent the problem.

Amniocentesis is a fairly safe procedure, but it does entail risks. Mild complications for the mother occur in only 2% or 3% of women. Less than 1% of women who undergo amniocentesis have miscarriages.

Chorionic villi sampling (CVS) can be done as early as the eighth week. In CVS, a tube is inserted through the vagina and cervix to the uterus. Small samples of tissue are taken from the tiny, hairlike villi on the membrane that surrounds the fetus. Testing these samples can re-

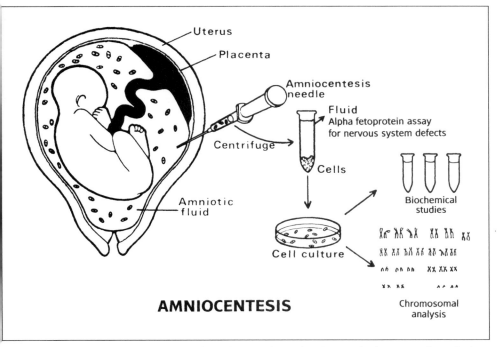

AMNIOCENTESIS

Amniocentesis is a prenatal test that can determine the sex of a fetus as well as whether the fetus carries certain genetic defects. Fetal chromosomes from amniotic fluid are shown here ordered and paired.

veal the same information as amniocentesis, but the results are known in only two days and are known much earlier in the pregnancy.

Ultrasound sonography is used to detect many birth defects, but it does not check for most genetic diseases. A sonograph uses ultrasonic (high frequency) waves to form a picture of the fetus. Sound waves are directed toward the fetus, and their echoes are converted into electrical signals printed as outlines on a television screen. These signals can be photographed and studied by the physician. The doctor can identify the size, shape, and location of structures in the uterus.

COMPLICATIONS DURING PREGNANCY

During the course of a pregnancy, many women experience some aches and pains. Most of these discomforts are not signs that anything is wrong. Backaches, fatigue, heartburn, and frequent urination are among the minor complaints associated with pregnancy. In fact, these symptoms rarely last long.

However, some conditions during pregnancy are potential dangers to both the mother and the fetus. If any of the symptoms of these conditions are present, they should be reported to a doctor as soon as possible.

Ectopic pregnancy is a rare complication in which the fertilized ovum develops in the fallopian tube instead of in the uterus. If untreated, the tube will eventually rupture, causing severe pain and bleeding. If an ectopic pregnancy is diagnosed, the doctor will surgically remove the affected tube. In most cases, having one tube does not affect the chances of a normal pregnancy in the future.

Toxemia is a condition that occurs most often during the last trimester of pregnancy. In the later months, some women develop high blood pressure, protein in their urine, and an excess of fluid in their tissues. Toxemia can interfere with the way in which the placenta does its job. It can be detected in its early, milder form during routine prenatal examinations. Toxemia patients have to control their weight and their blood pressure and are often advised to get a lot of bed rest.

Abruptio placentae involves the partial detachment of the placenta from the uterus before delivery. If the placenta detaches completely, the fetus will receive no food and oxygen. The symptoms of this condition include bleeding and pain over the uterus. If the placenta has detached only slightly, the doctor may wait it out. If the separation is advanced and there is bright red bleeding, the baby may have to be delivered early.

Placenta previa occurs in 1 out of 200 pregnancies. The placenta develops too low in the uterus, low enough to cover some or all of the opening to the cervix. If this condition is present, the baby has to be delivered by cesarean section.

Miscarriage, the spontaneous end of a pregnancy before the 28th week, has many causes. Miscarriages generally occur when there is a problem with the fetus or if it dies. In later miscarriages, the placenta may not have developed properly and cannot support a pregnancy. Miscarriages also may be the result of a condition in the mother. She may not produce enough of the hormones her body needs during pregnancy. She may have something wrong with her uterus, or she may have an infection in one of her reproductive organs.

The first sign of a miscarriage is usually vaginal bleeding. Sometimes, after bed rest, the bleeding stops and the threatened miscarriage does not take place. However, if a fetus is going to be miscarried, often nothing can be done to stop it. Most probably, the fetus has died in the uterus and will have to be expelled. After a miscarriage, a D&C may be necessary to remove any products of the pregnancy that are still in the uterus.

COMPLICATIONS DURING CHILDBIRTH

Sometimes a delivery does not go as smoothly as it might. When complications arise during childbirth, the doctor or midwife is prepared to step in and help the baby be born more easily and safely.

Sometimes it is necessary to speed up the delivery. Labor may go on for too long a time and may lead to problems for the mother or the baby. In such a situation, *forceps* may be used to help the baby through the birth canal. Forceps are metal instruments that look like tongs with handles. The blades of the forceps are curved to fit smoothly on each side of the baby's head. In the final stage of a delivery, the instrument can be inserted into the first inch or two of the vagina. Here it is used to help pull the baby forward or to turn its head into a better birth position.

A *ventouse* is another instrument that helps to gently pull the baby at birth. It is a shallow metal suction cup that is applied to the baby's head. The ventouse can be used at an earlier stage of labor than forceps.

Some babies cannot pass safely or easily through the birth canal. These babies will be delivered through an incision made in the abdominal wall and in the uterus. A cesarean section, or C-section, is a major surgical procedure. Often the doctor will determine early in the pregnancy that this is the safest way for the baby to be delivered. Other times, a complication may arise at the last minute, and the decision to perform a C-section is made after labor has already begun.

Just before birth, most babies have turned head down in the uterus, facing the mother's back. This *vertex* position is the easiest one for passing down the birth canal. However, not all babies are in this *presentation* when labor begins. *Malpresentations* include the *breech* position—backside or feet first—which occurs in 3% of deliveries. Sometimes the doctor is able to turn the baby into the head-down position before delivery. If the doctor feels that the breech position might slow the baby down, it may be decided that a C-section is the safest form of delivery. Some babies are in a head-down position but face the front of the mother's body rather than the back. The skull of a baby in this *posterior* position touches the mother's spine. As a result, she may feel labor

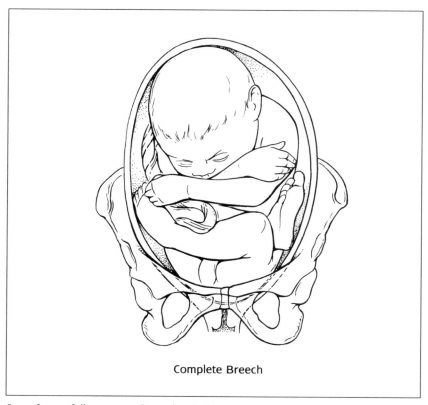

Complete Breech

Some fetuses fail to present themselves in the vertex, or head down, position that allows them to pass though the birth canal with the most ease. In a breech position the fetus is backside first and may have to be turned by the doctor or delivered via C-section.

pains in her back rather than her abdomen. Once in a great while, a baby will begin to turn and settle in a horizontal position, across the abdomen. The doctor may try to move the baby from this *transverse* position and coax it to complete its turn. If this cannot be done, the baby will have to be delivered by cesarean section.

CHILDBIRTH

Most mothers choose to have their babies in hospitals, attended by the doctor who cared for them during pregnancy. Some hospitals have special birthing rooms designed to look more like a home than a hospital. Other women choose a childbearing maternity center. These centers are

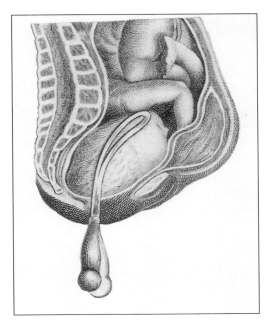

Instruments such as forceps are sometimes used to aid in the delivery of a baby. This engraving from a book on midwifery shows such a delivery.

run by nurses who are trained as midwives and usually are in close contact with maternity hospitals and physicians. Some women may choose to give birth in their own home with the help of a midwife or other professional.

Mothers-to-be can also learn how to make the experience of giving birth a little easier. They can attend classes that teach different methods to help them to relax during labor. Classes in *natural childbirth* teach special breathing exercises that lessen pain and special physical exercises that help the body to become more flexible.

A French obstetrician, Fernand Lamaze, developed a method designed to help a mother gain control over her labor. A pregnant woman usually attends Lamaze classes with her husband or partner, who acts as her coach. She learns how to relax her body muscles and how to position herself and breathe during labor.

LABOR AND DELIVERY

After 266 days of development and growth, the fetus is ready to be born. When the time is right, the mother's body prepares to help the fetus leave her body. She begins to push the baby through the birth canal. This is the beginning of labor. No two females experience labor in exactly the same way, but all experience three distinct stages of labor.

Before labor actually begins, other related events may take place. The fetus drops lower in the pelvis. Two weeks before labor, the cervix begins to shorten and thin out during *effacement.* After effacement, the mouth of the cervix also begins to open slightly, or dilate.

During pregnancy, a small wad of mucus closes off the cervical opening. During effacement, this plug may loosen and detach from the cervix, causing a thicker, deep pink or red discharge from the vagina. Another change takes place only in 1 out of 10 pregnancies. The amniotic sac breaks, and its warm fluid gushes out of the vagina. After a female *breaks her water,* labor is not far off.

During labor, the uterus reaches a point where it contracts rhythmically at regular intervals. The first stage of labor begins with the very first contraction. Early contractions are usually mild. They last around half a minute and occur 10 to 20 minutes apart. The contractions of the uterus get stronger, longer, and closer together. At the end of the first stage of labor, contractions may be two minutes apart and last up to a full minute. During this time, the cervix continues to efface until it is paper thin. The cervix also continues to dilate until it is about 10 centimeters, or 4 inches, wide. When the cervix is completely effaced and fully dilated, the mother usually is considered ready to deliver the baby.

During the second stage of labor, the contractions become strong enough to force the baby down and out. As the baby moves downward, the mother begins to bear down, or push along with the contractions. As most babies are born head down, the head gradually appears at the opening of the vagina. If the baby's head needs more room, the doctor or midwife may make a cut in the *perineum* (the skin between the labia and the anus). This incision, or *episiotomy,* makes it easier for the head to emerge.

Once the baby's head is out, its nose and mouth are cleared so it will be able to breathe. The shoulders follow the head, and very quickly the rest of the body slides out. At this point, the *umbilical cord,* which attaches the fetus to the placenta, is still connected to the baby and the placenta. As soon as the body is out, the doctor or midwife will clamp and cut the umbilical cord.

Somewhere in the middle of all this activity the baby will begin to cry. With this spontaneous act the baby takes his or her first breath of

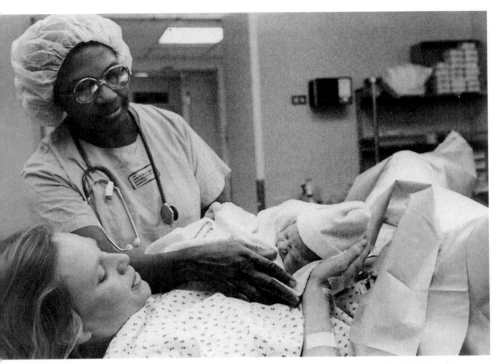

Although labor and delivery may be difficult for many women, seeing their newborn baby for the first time makes it seem more than worth the pain. The creation of this new life is the goal of both the male and female reproductive systems.

air. Eyedrops are placed in the baby's eyes to prevent infection. Often, vitamin K is given to new babies; their bodies cannot yet produce this nutrient, which is needed to prevent bleeding.

Right after the delivery, the third stage of labor begins. During this stage, the placenta separates from the wall of the uterus. The placenta and its membranes, the *afterbirth,* are now delivered. All of this material must be removed so that no bleeding problems develop. Some women receive medication to help the delivery of the placenta. Finally, if an episiotomy was necessary, it is stitched up.

At this point, pregnancy, labor, and childbirth are over, and the reproductive system has completed its remarkable job. A new life has been created and brought into the world. But the story is not finished. Whereas many other creatures can fend for themselves immediately after birth, human babies are quite helpless for many years to come. The work of mothers and fathers does not end with childbirth, but continues, and creates a rich and complex family life, full of the joys and frustrations of parenthood; and this more than anything else makes human beings what they are.

APPENDIX

FOR MORE INFORMATION

The following is a list of organizations that can provide information on issues related to the reproductive system.

General

American College Health Association
P.O. Box 28937
Baltimore, MD 21240
(410) 859-1500
www.acha.org

Food and Drug Administration
Office of Consumer Affairs
5600 Fishers Lane
Rockville, MD 20857
(888) INFO-FDA
www.fda.gov

Government Printing Office
Superintendent of Documents
Washington, DC 20402
(202) 512-1991
www.access.gpo.gov

National Health Information Center
Office of Disease Prevention and Health
  Promotion
U.S. Department of Health and Human
  Services
Washington, DC 20013-1133
(800) 336-4797
http://nhic-nt.health.org
(referrals to sources on specific topics)

National Maternal and Child Health
  Clearinghouse
(888) 434-4MCH

National Women's Health Network
514 10th Street NW, Suite 400
Washington, DC 20004
(202) 628-7814
www.womenshealthnetwork.org
(provides information on a number of
  topics related to reproduction and
  family planning)

Sex Information and Education Council
  of the United States (SIECUS)
130 West 42nd Street, Suite 350
New York, NY 10036
(212) 819-9770
www.siecus.org

Disorders of the Reproductive System

American College of Obstetricians and
  Gynecologists
409 12th Street SW
Washington, DC 20090
(202) 638-5577
www.acog.org

National Cancer Institute
Office of Cancer Communications
Building 31, Room 10A-03
31 Center Drive
Bethesda, MD 20892
(301) 435-3848
(800) 4-CANCER
www.nci.nih.gov

The Endometriosis Association
8585 North 76th Place
Milwaukee, WI 53223
(414) 355-2200 (in Wisconsin)
(800) 992-3636

Family Planning

Alan Guttmacher Institute
120 Wall Street
New York, NY 10005
(212) 248-1111
www.agi-usa.org

Family Service Association of America
333 Seventh Avenue
3rd Floor
New York, NY 10001
(212) 967-2740
(provides information and counseling
references on a number of topics
associated with family planning)

National Abortion Federation
1755 Massachusetts Avenue NW,
Suite 600
Washington, DC 20036
(202) 667-5881
Hot Line: (800) 772-9100
www.prochoice.org

Planned Parenthood Federation of
America
National Headquarters
810 Seventh Avenue
New York, NY 10019
(212) 541-7800
www.plannedparenthood.org
(provides information on sexually
transmitted diseases, pregnancy,
abortion, birth control, basic
gynecological care, and other related
topics; consult the telephone directory
for a local chapter)

Genetics and Birth Defects

Alliance of Genetic Support Groups
4301 Connecticut Avenue NW, Suite 404
Washington, DC 20008
(202) 966-5557
(800) 336-GENE
www.geneticalliance.org

Center for Birth Defects Information
Services
Dover Medical Building
Box 1176
Dover, MA 02030
(508) 785-2525

DES Action Canada
5890 Monkland, Suite 203
Montreal, Quebec H4A 1G2
Canada
(800) 4821-DES

DES Action USA
1615 Broadway, Suite 510
Oakland, CA 94612
(800) DES-9288
www.desact.org

March of Dimes Birth Defects
Foundation
1275 Mamaroneck Avenue
White Plains, NY 10605
(888)-MODIMES
www.modimes.org
(provides information on a number of
birth defects; also refers individuals to
local counseling services)

National Association for Sickle Cell
Disease
200 Corporate Pointe, Suite 495
Culver City, CA 90230
(800) 421-8453
www.sicklecelldisease.org

National Easter Seal Society
230 West Monroe Street, Suite 1800
Chicago, IL 60606
(800) 221-6827
www.easter-seals.org
(provides public health education and
funds both research and rehabilitation
services)

National Tay-Sachs and Allied Diseases
Association
2001 Beacon Street, Suite 204
Brighton, MA 02135
(800) 906-8723
www.ntsad.org

Pregnancy and Childbirth

Check the phone book under city, county, or state for Department of Health listings
for maternal and child health or maternity services and family planning. These
bureaus may be able to provide information on locally available prenatal care,
counseling, or childbirth classes.

American College of Nurse-Midwives
818 Connecticut Avenue NW, Suite 900
Washington, DC 20006
(202) 728-9897
www.acnm.org

American College of Obstetricians and
Gynecologists
409 12th Street SW
Washington, DC 20090
(202) 638-5577
www.acog.org

American Society for Psychoprophylaxis
in Obstetrics
Lamaze Method of Childbirth
1200 19th Street NW, Suite 300
Washington, DC 20036
(800) 368-4404
www.lamaze-childbrith.com

Childbirth Education Association
P.O. Box 58573
Cincinnati, OH 45258
(513) 661-5655
www.cininet.com/cea

International Childbirth Education
Association
P.O. Box 20048
Minneapolis, MN 55420
(800) 624-4934
www.icea.org
(provides information about publications
discussing pregnancy, childbirth, and
parenting)

National Institute of Child Health and
Human Development
National Institutes of Health
Bethesda, MD 20892
(301) 496-4000
www.nichd.nih.gov

Sexually Transmitted Diseases

Canadian AIDS Society
170 Laurier Avenue W, Suite 1101
Ottawa, ON K1P 5V5
Canada
(613) 230-3580

THE REPRODUCTIVE SYSTEM

Centers for Disease Control
Department of Health and Human Services
Public Health Information Service
1600 Clifton Road NE
Atlanta, GA 30333
(800) 311-3435
www.cdc.gov

National AIDS Hotline
(800) 342-AIDS
www.cdc.gov

National Sexually Transmitted Disease
  Hotline
(800) 227-8922

APPENDIX

FURTHER READING

GENERAL

Bender, Stephanie DeGraff, and Kathleen Keileher. *PMS—A Positive Program to Gain Control.* Tucson, AZ: Body Press, 1986.

Buchsbaum, Herbert J. *The Menopause.* New York: Springer-Verlag, 1983.

DeCherney, Alan H. *Reproductive Failure.* New York: Churchill, 1986.

Farley, John. *Gametes and Spores: Ideas About Sexual Reproduction.* Baltimore: Johns Hopkins University Press, 1982.

Genazzani, A. R. *The Brain and Female Reproductive Function.* Park Ridge, NJ: Parthenon, 1988.

Gosden, R. G. *Biology of Menopause: The Causes and Consequences of Ovarian Aging.* New York: Academic Press, 1985.

Gruhn, John G. *Hormonal Regulation of the Menstrual Cycle: The Evolution of Concepts.* New York: Plenum, 1989.

Madaras, Lynda. *The What's Happening to My Body Book for Boys: A Growing Up Guide for Parents and Sons.* New York: Newmarket Press, 1987.

Madaras, Lynda. *The What's Happening to My Body Book for Girls: A Growing Up Guide for Parents and Daughters.* New York: Newmarket Press, 1987.

Mann, T., and C. Lutwak-Mann. *Male Reproductive Function and Semen.* New York: Springer-Verlag, 1981.

Miller, Jonathan, and David Pelham. *The Facts of Life.* New York: Viking Press, 1984.

Nachtigall, Lila. *Estrogen: The Facts Can Change Your Life.* New York: Harper, 1995.

Negro-Vilar, Andres. *Male Reproduction and Fertility.* New York: Raven Press, 1983.

Older, Julia. *Endometriosis.* New York: Scribners, 1984.

Sloane, Ethel. *Biology of Women.* New York: Wiley, 1993.

Steinberger, Anna, and Emil Steinberger. *Testicular Development: Structure and Function.* New York: Raven Press, 1980.

Swanson, Janice, and Katherine Forrest. *Men's Reproductive Health.* New York: Springer, 1984.

FAMILY PLANNING

Bertacchi, Gloria M. *Birth Control Choices.* Rev. ed. Fair Oaks, CA: National Medical Seminars, 1988.

Breitman, Patti, et al. *How to Persuade Your Lover to Use a Condom . . . and Why You Should.* 2nd ed. Rocklin, CA: Prima, 1994.

Canape, Charlene. *Adoption: Parenthood Without Pregnancy.* New York: Henry Holt & Co., 1986.

Chalker, Rebecca. *Complete Cervical Cap Guide: Everything You Want to Know About This Safe, Effective, No-Mess, Time-Tested Birth Control Option.* New York: Harper & Row, 1987.

Dickey, Richard. *Oral Contraceptive User Guide.* Durant, OK: Creative Informatics, 1987.

Hafez, E. S. *Voluntary Termination of Pregnancy.* Norwell, MA: Klawer Academic, 1984.

Hatcher, Robert A., et al. *Contraceptive Technology.* 17th ed. New York: Irvington, 1998.

Hodgson, Jane E. *Abortion and Sterilization: Medical and Social Aspects.* Orlando, FL: Grune, 1981.

Wolkind, Stephen. *Medical Aspects of Adoption and Foster Care.* Philadelphia: Lippincott, 1980.

World Health Organization. *Barrier Contraceptives and Spermicides: Their Role in Family Planning Care.* Albany: World Health Organization, 1987.

GENETIC DISORDERS

Carter, Thomas P., and Ann M. Wiley. *Genetic Disease: Screening and Management.* New York: Alan R. Liss, 1985.

Gardner, R. J., and G. R. Sutherland. *Chromosome Abnormalities and Genetic Counseling.* 2nd ed. New York: Oxford University Press, 1996.

Milunsky, Aubrey. *Genetic Disorders and the Fetus: Diagnosis, Prevention, and Treatment.* 4th ed. Baltimore: Johns Hopkins University Press, 1998.

Porter, Ian H., et al. *Perinatal Genetics: Diagnosis and Treatment.* San Diego: Academic Press, 1986.

Romero, Robert, et al. *Prenatal Diagnosis of Congenital Anomalies.* New York: McGraw-Hill, 1997.

PREGNANCY AND CHILDBIRTH

Epps, Roselyn. *The American Medical Women's Association Guide to Pregnancy and Childbirth.* New York: Dell, 1996.

Feinbloom, Richard I. *Pregnancy, Birth, and the Early Months: A Complete Guide.* 2nd ed. New York: Perseus, 1993.

Fuchs, Fritz. *Endocrinology of Pregnancy.* 3rd ed. New York: Harper & Row, 1983.

Tanner, James M. *Foetus into Man: Physical Growth from Conception to Maturity.* Cambridge: Harvard University Press, 1990.

Tapley, Donald F., and W. Duane Todd. *The Columbia University College of Physicians and Surgeons Guide to Pregnancy.* New York: Crown, 1988.

SEXUALLY TRANSMITTED DISEASES

Balfour, Henry H. *Herpes Diseases and Your Health.* Minneapolis: University of Minnesota Press, 1984.

Brooks, George F. *Gonococcal Infection.* Baltimore: E. Arnold, 1985.

Haraw, Sam J. *Pathology and Pathophysiology of AIDS and HIV-Related Diseases.* St. Louis, MO: Mosby, 1989.

Madaras, Lynda. *Lynda Madaras Talks to Teens about AIDS: An Essential Guide for Parents, Teachers, and Young People.* New York: Newmarket, 1988.

Morse, Stephen, et al. *Atlas of Sexually Transmitted Diseases.* 2nd ed. St. Louis, MO: Mosby, 1996.

Nahmias, Andre J. *Bacteria, Mycoplasmae, Chlamydiae, and Fungi.* New York: Plenum, 1981.

Reeve, Peter. *Chlamydial Infections.* New York: Springer-Verlag, 1987.

Schell, Ronald F. *Pathology and Immunology of Treponemal Infection.* New York: Dekker, 1983.

APPENDIX

GLOSSARY

Afterbirth: The placenta and other fetal membranes expelled from the uterus after childbirth.

Amniocentesis: A prenatal test in which a needle is inserted through the abdominal wall into the uterus of a pregnant female to obtain amniotic fluid, which contains fetal cells; these cells are used to determine the sex of the fetus and abnormalities in fetal chromosomes.

Asexual reproduction: Process of producing offspring without the involvement of sex cells, as by fission or budding.

Balanoposthitis: Balanitis; inflammation of the upper part of the penis and underlying mucous membrane.

Blastula: Spherical structure of cells produced by cleavage of a fertilized ovum; consists of a single layer of cells, called the blastoderm, that surrounds a fluid-filled cavity, or blastocoel.

Candidiasis: A type of vaginitis; an infection of the moist cutaneous areas of the body, including the mouth, intestinal tract, skin, and vagina, caused by an excess of *Candida,* a yeastlike fungus that is commonly part of the normal flora in those areas.

Cervical erosion: Process in which cells from the inner lining of the cervix spread and cover the tip of the cervix, which may result in irritation, infection, and possibly bleeding or discharge.

Cesarean section: Delivery of the fetus by incision in the abdominal walls and uterus.

Chorionic villi sampling: A prenatal test in which a tube is inserted through the vagina and into the uterus, where small samples of tissue are taken from the villi of the chorion, a membrane that surrounds the fetus; used to determine the sex of the fetus and abnormalities in fetal chromosomes.

Circumcision: Surgical removal of all or part of the prepuce, or foreskin; performed for hygienic and religious reasons.

Cyst: Closed cavity, or sac, containing a fluid, semifluid, or solid material; caused by developmental anomalies, blockage of ducts, or parasitic infection.

D&C: Dilation and curettage; process of dilating, or expanding, the cervix, then scraping cells from the wall of the uterus, used to test for cell abnormalities, to remove growths, or as a form of abortion.

DES: Diethylstilbestrol; a synthetic form of estrogen that is several times more potent than the natural hormone; used to treat menopausal symptoms and other estrogen-related deficiencies; has been linked to severe birth defects and vaginal malignancies.

Endometriosis: Disease in which the tissue of the uterine mucous membrane, called the endometrium, migrates to other areas and grows by responding to the changing levels of hormones that control the menstrual cycle; can result in bleeding, internal scarring, and other complications.

Epididymitis: Inflammation of the epididymus, the small oblong structure with a coiled duct located on the outward and central part of the scrotum that provides a place for storage and maturation of sperm and a path for transit of sperm.

Episiotomy: Incision into the vagina and perineum, the external region between the vulva and the anus, before childbirth to prevent tearing of the perineum and to facilitate delivery.

ERT: Estrogen replacement therapy; controversial treatment in which estrogen supplements are prescribed to relieve menopausal symptoms and reduce osteoporosis, a gradual thinning of the bones.

Estrogen: Sex hormone produced by the ovaries responsible for the development of secondary sex characteristics and for cyclic changes in the vaginal endothelium and epithelium.

Fetal membrane: One of several structures, including the allantois, amnion, chorion, and placenta, that serve to protect and support the fetus or embryo.

Fibroid: Fibroma; benign tumor made up of fibrous and or fully developed connective tissue.

FSH: Follicle-stimulating hormone; gonadotropic hormone produced in the anterior pituitary gland; in conjunction with luteinizing hormone, controls the secretion of sex hormones and the production of sperm and eggs.

Gamete: A mature reproductive cell; called the ovum in females and the sperm in males.

HCG: Human chorionic gonadotropin; a hormone produced by the placenta; can be detected in urine a few days after conception, thus providing a way to confirm pregnancy.

Hormone: A chemical substance transported by the bloodstream that has a specific regulatory effect on certain organs of the body.

Hypospadias: A congenital abnormality in which the urethra opens on the underside of the penis; in female hypospadias the urethra opens into the vagina.

Hypothalamus: Area at the base of the brain that secretes hormones that regulate reproduction, metabolism, and behavioral responses.

Hysterectomy: Surgical removal of part or all of the uterus; performed most frequently for the purpose of removing benign or malignant tumors.

LH: Luteinizing hormone; a sex hormone produced in the hypothalamus that stimulates the ovaries to release an egg into the fallopian tube.

Lumpectomy: Surgical removal of a cancerous growth from the breast.

Mammography: An X-ray study of the breasts used for the early detection of cancer.

Meiosis: Cell division forming gametes, which have half the number of chromosomes characteristic of the somatic, or body, cells of the species.

Menopause: The natural cessation of menstruation, usually occurring between the ages of 45 and 50; may be accompanied by hot flashes, feeling of weakness, and in some cases depression.

Menorrhagia: Excessive uterine bleeding during menstruation, the flow being greater than usual either in volume, number of days, or both.

Menstruation: The periodic shedding of the uterine lining in the absence of pregnancy.

Miscarriage: Spontaneous abortion; loss and expulsion of the fetus or embryo before it is viable, or able to survive outside of the mother's body on its own.

Morula: Solid mass of cells formed by cleavage of a fertilized ovum.

Orchitis: An infection brought to the testes by the bloodstream; marked by pain, swelling, and a feeling of heaviness.

Ovariectomy: Oophorectomy; removal of a portion of an ovary, a whole ovary, or both ovaries.

Ovulation: Release of an egg cell, or ovum, from an ovary into the oviduct.

Palpation: Examination by the application of pressure with hands or fingers to the external surface of the body to detect disease or abnormalities within the body.

Pap smear: Pap, or Papanicolaou, test; study of cells taken from the cervix and vagina to evaluate endocrine function and to diagnose malignancies.

Paraphimosis: Retraction of narrowed or inflamed prepuce, or foreskin, that can cause strangulation of the end of the penis.

PID: Pelvic inflammatory disease; any pelvic infection ascending into the female's upper genital tract beyond the cervix.

Pineal gland: A cone-shaped glandlike structure in the brain whose exact function remains unknown.

Pituitary gland: A small gland located in the brain and attached to the hypothalamus; controls the thyroid, adrenal, and sex glands.

PMS: Premenstrual syndrome; physical and emotional condition caused by a rise and fall in hormonal levels during the course of the menstrual cycle; common symptoms include soreness, bloating, tension, and irritability.

Priapism: Abnormal, painful, sustained erection of the penis; accompanies diseases and injuries to the spinal cord.

Progesterone: Steroid hormone produced in the corpus luteum, the adrenal glands, or the placenta; responsible for the changes in the endometrium during the second half of the menstrual cycle that prepare the uterus for pregnancy.

Prolapse: Downward displacement of the uterus resulting from weakening of the ligaments that normally hold the uterus in place.

Prostatitis: Inflammation of the prostate gland; may be a complication of gonorrheal infection or a long-standing bacterial infection.

Puerperal fever: Childbed fever; infection that follows childbirth as a result of the tearing of the mucous membrane that lines the birth canal.

Salpingitis: Inflammation of the fallopian tube caused by either gonorrheal or other bacterial infection.

Sex chromosomes: Those chromosomes associated with the determination of gender; the X and Y chromosomes in mammals.

Sexual reproduction: Act or process of producing offspring with the involvement of sex cells; the combination of a male sex cell, or sperm, with a female sex cell, or ovum.

Sims' position: The semiprone position in which a patient is placed during vaginal examination or treatment so that she is lying on her left side with right knee and thigh drawn in toward her chest and left arm lying parallel to her back.

Smegma: Thick, cheesy, odoriferous secretion of the sebaceous glands found under the labia of females and the foreskin of males.

Testosterone: Sex hormone produced in both men and women; influences sexual behavior and is responsible for secondary sex characteristics.

Thermography: Use of a photographic device that detects and records, through infrared radiation, heat present in surface areas of the body; shows the flow of blood to limbs and helps detect cancer.

TSS: Toxic shock syndrome; severe illness characterized by high fever, vomiting, and diarrhea; thought to be caused by a bacterial infection that occurs almost exclusively in menstruating women.

Ultrasonography: Ultrasound; the visualization of the body's structures or a growing fetus or embryo by recording the reflections of pulses of ultrasonic waves directed into the body.

Umbilical cord: The attachment that connects the fetus with the placenta through which the fetus receives nourishment from and excretes waste through the mother's bloodstream; when severed after birth, leaves a depression on the abdomen of the child called a navel, or umbilicus.

Undescended testicles: Developmental defect in the fetal stage of males in which the testes fail to descend from the abdominal cavity into the scrotum.

Vaginitis: Inflammation of the vagina marked by pain and discharge; may be caused by bacteria, strong chemicals, deficiency of vitamins, or an estrogen deficiency in postmenopausal women.

Zygote: Fertilized ovum; produced by the union of a male and female gamete.

APPENDIX

INDEX

APPENDIX

PICTURE CREDITS

13: The Bettmann Archive

15: Dave Woodward/Taurus Photos

16: From Fundamental Concepts of Modern Biology by Sebastian Haskel and David Sygoda, copyright 1972 by Amsco School Publications, Inc., New York

18: Children's Defense Fund

21: National Library of Medicine

24: The Bettmann Archive

27: National Library of Medicine

32: Original illustrations by Gary Tong

37: David M. Phillips/The Population Council 1986/Taurus Photos

40: Original illustrations by Gary Tong

47: David Phillips/ Taurus Photos

50: Original illustrations by Robert Margulies

53: Original illustrations by Robert Margulies

63: Centers for Disease Control

68: National Library of Medicine

70: Centers for Disease Control

73: Martin M. Rotker/Taurus Photos

75: Copyright Frank Siteman/Taurus Photos

78: AP/Wide World Photos

82: Shirley Zeiberg/Taurus Photos

85: Copyright Don Rutledge 1981/Taurus Photos

87: Original illustrations by Robert Margulies

89: Original illustrations by Gary Tong

97: National Institutes of Health

100: Original illustrations by Robert Margulies

101: The Bettmann Archive

103: Copyright Eric Kroll 1984/Taurus Photos

Regina Avraham has been a science teacher with the New York City Board of Education since the 1960s. She also edits and writes textbooks and general-interest books for young adults. Ms. Avraham currently teaches biology and coordinates a science magnet program in New York City.

Sandra L. Thurman, a graduate of Mercer University, is the Director of the Office of National AIDS Policy at the White House. For more than a decade, Ms. Thurman has been a leader and advocate for people with AIDS at the local, state, and federal levels. From 1988 to 1993, Ms. Thurman served as the Executive Director of AID Atlanta, a community-based nonprofit organization that provides health and support services to people living with HIV/AIDS. From 1993 to 1996, Ms. Thurman was the Director of Advocacy Programs at the Task Force for Child Survival and Development at the Carter Center in Atlanta, Georgia. Most recently, she served as the Director of Citizen Exchanges at the United States Information Agency. She is a recognized expert on AIDS issues and has provided testimony before the United States Senate, the White House Conference on HIV/AIDS, and the National Commission on AIDS.

C. Everett Koop, M.D., Sc.D., currently serves as chairman of the board of his own website, www.drkoop.com, and is the Elizabeth DeCamp McInerny professor at Dartmouth College, from which he graduated in 1937. Dr. Koop received his doctor of medicine degree from Cornell Medical College in 1941 and his doctor of science degree from the University of Pennsylvania in 1947. A pediatric surgeon of international reputation, he was previously surgeon in chief of Children's Hospital of Philadelphia and professor of pediatric surgery and pediatrics at the University of Pennsylvania. A former U.S. Surgeon General, Dr. Koop was also the director of the Office of International Health. He has served as surgery editor of the *Journal of Clinical Pediatrics* and editor in chief of the *Journal of Pediatric Surgery*. In his more than 60 years of experience in health care, government, and industry, Dr. Koop has received numerous awards and honors, including 35 honorary degrees.